Startup Seed Funding for the Rest of Us

*How to Raise $1 Million For Your Startup –
Even Outside of Silicon Valley*

By Mike Belsito

TABLE OF CONTENTS

INTRODUCTION

Many entrepreneurs call Silicon Valley the land of opportunity. It is there that the dreams of hatching an idea for a technology startup and accessing a million dollars of seed funding not only exist, but they are actually a reality. There's no single place in the world that has a greater concentration of angel and venture capital investors. These investors are all looking to write checks to the next Mark Zuckerberg or Evan Spiegel. First-time founders in Silicon Valley enjoy a place where failure is considered a "badge of honor," and where potential co-founders, lead investors, and even acquirers all might be found in a local café.

And then, there are the rest of us.

This book is specifically written for founders, especially first-timers, who have the same dreams and aspirations as their peers in Silicon Valley. They want to see their technologies brought to life. They see themselves as problem solvers for consumers and business enterprises. They want to "disrupt" traditional business models through the use of technology.

There's just one big difference. They're from Cleveland, or Detroit, or Kansas City, Tampa, Albuquerque, Boise, Hartford, or any other "non-traditional" startup community.

In places like these, raising money to fund a startup can seem like such a foreign concept. There typically isn't a hotbed of angel investors and venture capitalists just waiting to write checks.

For the investors that do exist, their risk profile is usually much more conservative than those willing to make bets in Silicon Valley and their preference is to invest in what they know. Often times, this doesn't include consumer Internet companies or software-as-a-service businesses. While it may be a challenge for founders in Silicon Valley to access funding for their startup, it seems downright impossible for those founders outside of the Bay Area.

Yet, despite the obstacles, it's *not* impossible for founders outside of Silicon Valley to find the funding they need. My experience launching eFuneral in Cleveland, Ohio proved that to be true, as we raised nearly $1 Million for our Internet startup company. On paper, my co-founder and I shouldn't have received this funding:

We didn't have previous experience starting and selling companies for a profit.

We weren't operating in a "hot" industry. In fact, we operated in the world of funeral services, a field that was not known for attracting the interest of venture capitalists.

We weren't located in Silicon Valley – or even any of the next-tier startup communities such as New York, Austin, Boulder, or Los Angeles. We were in Cleveland, Ohio.

We had no previous experience in the industry we were building our product for. My co-founder and I didn't grow up working in "the funeral business", and, thankfully, we hadn't planned too many funeral services for friends or family members in our lifetime – although a personal experience is what led to the conception of eFuneral.

Despite of all of this, we were able to raise nearly $1 million in startup seed funding and became one of the most talked about startup companies in our community.

When I reflect on how we accomplished this, I realize that while many of the things we did to lead us to funding were done intentionally, some were mere luck. This book was written so that you can learn about the path we took, understand what worked, and incorporate what we learned from our experiences into your startup journey. Yet, the stories don't just stop with my own personal experiences. This book incorporates information and advice from a collection of founders outside of Silicon Valley who have successfully raised startup capital, as well as the investors who have funded them.

If you're reading this and you *are* located in Silicon Valley –
you're still likely to find useful advice throughout this book that will
be relevant to raising a seed round for your startup. But this book
wasn't really written for you. This book was written for the
entrepreneur who faces challenges each day specific to raising
funds *outside* of Silicon Valley.

A Word of Caution

If you're expecting that reading this book is a surefire guarantee
that you'll be able to raise millions of dollars in funding for your
startup simply by learning a few simple tricks, you're likely to be
disappointed. It took a lot of hard work that spanned many months of
sleepless nights and near breakdowns. However, this book is designed
to help you understand what works well so you can effectively put
yourself on a faster and more likely path to finding the funding that
you need. If you're willing to have an open mind, take action, and
understand that raising startup capital is a process – not a single action
item – this book will be a helpful companion throughout your journey.

Resources

Throughout the book, you'll notice me reference several other
books, websites, and other helpful resources. I've taken the time to
collate all of these resources into a single, downloadable guide that
you can access for free at: SeedFundingBook.com/FreeResources.

PROLOGUE (MY STORY)

My first startup

I was standing in front of the Veale Center athletic complex at Case Western Reserve University in Cleveland, Ohio. I was about to pitch my first startup. I didn't realize it at that moment. In fact, I didn't realize that I was actually starting *any* type of business at the time - if I did I may have been nervous. I thought I'd be having a casual conversation with CWRU's Athletics Director about a possible internship. What ensued was a conversation that would determine how I would live the rest of my life.

I was just coming off of my graduation from Bowling Green State University when I was accepted into the MBA program at the Weatherhead School of Management at CWRU. CWRU is located in my hometown of Cleveland, Ohio. At this point in my career, my professional goal was to become a Division 1 Intercollegiate Athletics Director. With the eight sports-related internships I had during my time at BGSU, I had prepared myself as best I could to pursue my dream. When I was accepted at Weatherhead, I was excited to add a ninth internship in CWRU's Athletics department to my resume.

So there I stood, waiting for my appointment with CWRU's Athletics Director. When the clock struck two o'clock, I entered the building and took a deep breath. I wasn't just going to ask for an internship; I actually had a specific game plan in mind. I wanted to join her staff in helping bring in Corporate Sponsorships for the Athletic Department. A recent internship where I was exposed to this type of fundraising got me thinking about taking what I've learned and implementing it at my new campus.

I was greeted by Kristin Hughes, an athlete in her own right who served as the Athletics Director as well as the Women's Basketball Coach. Having only exchanged emails until this point, I was pretty certain that Kristin did not know what to expect from me. After introducing myself, I explained to Kristin that I wanted to help her by selling Corporate Sponsorships to local businesses.

"That would be great, Mike" she started, "but there's just one problem. We don't sell Corporate Sponsorships. Our staff is too busy with everything else that needs to get done, and we don't have enough money to hire somebody to focus on Corporate Sponsorships."

Of all the possible responses, I hadn't expected that one. I assumed that *all* athletics departments sold corporate sponsorships as a way to supplement revenue. Of the eight internships I had completed, three of them were with Division 1 intercollegiate athletics programs, all of which boasted well-developed sponsorship programs that generated much needed cash. As a Division 3 school, CWRU's limited budget was keeping them from starting a corporate sponsorship program, yet not having a corporate sponsorship program was holding them back from generating additional funds.

I quickly threw out the first thing that came to my mind. "Let *me* start it. I'll handle everything – and you can just pay me a percentage of whatever I'm able to raise. There won't be any risk."

Kristin smiled, "Interesting... I will think about that."

As it turned out, luck was on my side. It was one of Kristin's first days on the job as the Athletics Director and, as such, she was in a position to try something new. Perhaps my last-minute pitch was the quick-win the newly minted executive of the Athletics program was looking for. A couple of days later, I got a phone call from Kristin formally approving my proposal; she was going to let me build CWRU's Corporate Sponsorship program from scratch.

My first startup was born.

From sports to startups

Eighteen months later and a few months shy of graduation, I had a case of "MBA senioritis." My *real* professional life was about to begin and I was having doubts. On the one hand, my streak of sports-related internships had continued nicely and I could certainly continue down the sports track, as the corporate sponsorship program I created turned out to be a success. On the other hand, this new position allowed me to discover what it felt like to *create* something and I wondered how I could focus on this as a profession. I wondered if there might be a way to join a team of successful entrepreneurs who were creating a business from scratch, and would allow me to learn from them. Working as a one-man-operation at CWRU had been okay, but it was lonely; I probably made a lot of dumb mistakes that could have been avoided had I had partners to talk to, strategize with, and learn from. Then, in the most unlikely of places, I found the opportunity I was looking for.

Finding Findaway

One of the things that I was taught in Business School is that the best jobs are never posted. Leveraging your personal and professional network is what really helps you land that next great job. It turns out they were wrong, at least in this case.

It was through an online job posting that I found an opportunity to work with Findaway, which described itself as a "digital audio startup company." I met with Findaway's three co-founders, Christopher Celeste, Blake Squires, and Mitch Kroll. After a series of meetings, they made me a formal offer to join their team, which I accepted (not really knowing what I was getting myself into). We were attempting to create "physical digital audio books." We were going to have to create, market, brand, and launch a completely new format of books into the world. With the advent of the iPod, companies like Apple and Audible.com were getting into the digital audio book market. By most people's standards, trying to compete using a physical product when digital downloads were beginning to be in vogue seemed crazy. Many people thought we were betting on old technology using an outdated business model, but I didn't care. I believed in the founders and wanted to be a part of what *they* were doing.

I arrived on my first day ready to accept any challenge. When I sat at my desk, my business cards were waiting for me. My official title printed on the cards: Findawayer.

Learning from Findaway

Joining Findaway was the best thing that could have ever happened to me. At that point in my career, it was absolutely the right move. I became Employee #1 at a company with big ambitions that was also taking big risks. Initially, we were a very small team, which meant that wearing many hats was a must. There were times where I had to clean the conference room, make copies, and perform all sorts of other unglamorous tasks. But the best thing about it was that the CEO was right there next to me doing the same thing. Nobody was above doing whatever the business required. That, I learned, is what a true startup team is about.

Our product, a device called Playaway, was a pre-loaded digital audio player containing one book per device. It ran on a AAA battery and could be listened to over and over again. When somebody was done listening, they could put it on their shelf or give it to a friend just like a physical book or audio book on CD.

My main focus was to explore non-traditional channels where our product might be suitable. The co-founders had already negotiated agreements with major publishers and retailers prior to me joining the team. So I experimented quite a bit with other channels. Some of my initial customers included a 5 star resort in Mexico, a vending machine company that sold high-end electronics in airports, and other non-traditional channels. In the course of experimenting with a variety of these channels, I managed to land a meeting that would forever change the future of Findaway. It was with a public library, a channel that our business plan had totally ignored.

Nobody in our company knew anything about selling to libraries. None of us had even grasped the potential sales volume that libraries could offer. Yet, during my first meeting with a Collection Development Manager at one of the public libraries near our office, I realized that we were onto something big.

"So you're saying that the entire book is on this device, and we could loan it again and again to our patrons?" she asked.

"Well yes, technically you could," I responded, not yet knowing the magnitude of what Playaway's ability to be circulated multiple times would mean for our business.

She went on to explain to me that we actually solved a big problem for her and her library. Audio books on CD were one of the most circulated items at not only her library, but at *all* libraries. The problem, however, was that one audio book might consist of 10-15 individual CD's, and if one of those disks got scratched, they would have to take the entire audio book out of circulation. If our product was as durable as it seemed, it would help save them money.

That single meeting paved the way for Playaway to circulate in over 20,000 libraries and schools throughout the United States. Library and school sales ended up dwarfing our retail sales. Over the course of 5 years, Findaway grew to become a company that would generate more than $20M annually – with double-digit growth each year.

And, of course, as the company grew, I grew within the company. I eventually helped build and lead a sales team as the company's National Sales Manager. Leading our sales team was equal parts challenging and rewarding. It required me to manage people for the very first time. Being a young manager overseeing many people who were twice my age and had three or four times more experience wasn't easy. There were definitely bumps in the road. I bounced ideas off other managers in the company and sought guidance from them when needed. One of my favorite people to talk to was our Creative Director, Kurt Pettit – somebody who, like me, was relatively young and was tasked with managing a high performing group. Before long, we realized that we had a lot more in common than we thought.

Side Startup: Appstand

Kurt never had any shortage of creative ideas. I liked this about Kurt because it was something we had in common. When Findaway announced an office reorganization, Kurt and I asked if we could share an office. Sharing office space led to brainstorming and sharing of ideas. And in time, some of those ideas would lead us to opportunities outside of the scope of what we were doing at Findaway.

One day I shared an idea that I had with Kurt about a picture frame that somebody could slide an iPhone into while sitting at a desk. It would be a simple product – an inexpensive iPhone accessory. Instead of just talking about this, Kurt said, "Let's just *do* it. Let's see if we can actually make it happen."

We approached the co-founders of Findaway to ask for permission to work on developing a side product that we tentatively were calling Appstand. They agreed, so long as it didn't get in the way of our primary responsibilities at work. We worked early mornings and late nights on our side business, and in seven months' time, we were able to create a real, salable product. We had the product manufactured overseas and sold it into niche retail establishments like airport gadget shops, independent electronics stores, and online boutiques. We even received a positive review from David Pogue of the New York Times.

We quickly sold out of our first inventory run of Appstand units, and invested the money we earned into making a second batch. The second batch became more difficult for us to sell than we had imagined. Our momentum had died, the stores we did manage to sell into were curious about the *next* product we were developing. Bigger retail chains wanted to see *multiple* products from vendors in order to continue the relationship.

The thing was – we didn't really *want* to be iPhone accessory makers. We really just wanted to challenge ourselves to see if we could make something from scratch. Continuing on with Appstand would require more investment – and a much bigger time commitment, which we weren't prepared to make. So, our Appstand experiment came to an end. I viewed it as a major success. It gave us the confidence to know we absolutely could bring something to life on our own.

Shift to Product

Meanwhile, at Findaway, my Appstand experience was unexpectedly about to become very relevant. I soon shifted within the organization to a newly created product group and became our Product

Innovation Manager. In that role, I teamed up with several other Findawayers, including Bryan Chaikin, the company's first software engineer. Together, we launched several new products for our school and library customers.

At this stage, things were going great for both Bryan and me. We were doing interesting, yet challenging things at work. We were producing great products for our company. And after six years at a startup company, we were finally starting to get rewarded financially. We were also both newlyweds and were beginning to think about starting families of our own.

But then, out of nowhere something happened that changed my life. My cousin Ed died.

Ed's Death

I was lounging on the couch at home with my wife one Sunday afternoon when the phone rang. It was my stepmother. She called to let me know that my cousin Ed had died suddenly at the age of 43. No one was sure what had happened, just that my Aunt – his mother – found him inside of his house on the floor unresponsive. My Aunt was understandably devastated, and my Dad rushed to his sister's house to be by her side.

This period of time for us, as it most likely is for all families in this predicament, was very stressful. Decisions had to be made very quickly. We had to choose a funeral home to work with and decide on all of the arrangements for the service.

My Aunt was struggling to cope with her son's death, and didn't want to think about all of the details. My father agreed to make the arrangements but quickly became overwhelmed by the number of funeral homes to choose from – there are six funeral homes just within a few miles of my Aunt's house. "Mike, isn't there anything online that can help us find out how much these funeral homes cost and figure out which one is better than the other?" he asked me.

I assumed that there had to be something like this, especially since you can find information like this online for nearly *anything*. I was shocked to find out what little information there was on the Internet. At best, some websites provided contact details for area funeral homes with no more information than what a phone book would provide. Of course, we weren't simply looking for contact information. We were looking for information that we could use to actually make a *decision*.

We didn't have time to visit all six local funeral homes. My family simply picked one, and hoped for the best. I attended Ed's service with my wife, and fortunately, everything worked out just fine. Afterwards, my wife and I wanted to grab something to eat nearby. Being somewhat unfamiliar with the neighborhood we were in, I used a mobile app on my phone to pull up recommendations and reviews for nearby restaurants. When we sat down to eat, I had a revelation.

It dawned on me that we had online access to more information regarding restaurants, where checks average around $50, than we did about funeral homes where our total spending was upwards of $10,000.

I had no idea that the revelation I made would lead to me starting a business.

Beginning to learn about death care

The next week, I walked into my office at Findaway and saw Bryan coding at his desk. I blurted out, "the funeral industry is definitely messed up."

He raised his eyebrows, and responded, "I'm hearing an idea brewing…"

That casual observation led to Bryan and I deciding that we should explore this problem together, as we hoped to find a solution together. After a couple of months of research on our own, we began to engage a couple of my personal mentors, including Christopher – who had since moved on from Findaway – and Tim Mueller, and they both encouraged us to dig deeper. Like two young detectives hot on a new case, we were pouring through everything we could get our hands on to understand the industry. Christopher made a simple, yet profound, suggestion: "Go talk to people. Forget the numbers, you know them now. Go talk to families and funeral homes."

We followed his suggestion, and began meeting with people who had the unfortunate experience of recently having planned a funeral for a loved one. We also met with funeral directors to try to understand their perspective. We confirmed many of our original assumptions. Families did find the funeral planning process complicated and often *didn't* know which funeral home to turn to. Funeral directors shared with us that they spent a great deal – sometimes up to 20% of their expected revenue – on marketing, yet didn't have a great way to track their ROI. We were definitely onto something.

10xelerator Opportunity

The early morning and evening work sessions continued as Bryan and I learned more and more about the market that industry experts called "Death Care." We were running ourselves ragged but we thought that the opportunity was worth it.

Right about this time, an email appeared in my inbox announcing the State of Ohio's first foray into the accelerator business, following in the footsteps of Y-Combinator and Techstars. The State was about to run a pilot accelerator program called "the 10xelerator" in Columbus, Ohio, and was offering a $20,000 grant and mentorship from Ohio-based entrepreneurs, angel investors, and venture capitalists. The objective was to enable ten technology startups to accomplish a year's worth of work in just a ten-week period. This was our opportunity.

I shared the email with Bryan, and we both agreed that this could be our leaping-off point. We hadn't been ready to quit our full time jobs to pursue our new venture quite yet. But if the State of Ohio would validate us by accepting us into the program, perhaps we really were onto something. Plus, the worst-case scenario would be that we would enter the program and realize after three months that we were crazy. We both felt that we could find new jobs if we needed to and that the $20,000 would be enough to sustain us (and our families) for 90 days.

We sought guidance from Christopher and Tim. They upped the ante. They said that if we were able to land a spot in the 10xelerator class, they would personally be willing to match the amount we'd receive in the form of an investment they'd make in our company. The challenge was on.

I spent the afternoon of Easter 2011 completing our application to join the 10xelerator's first class. I explained the initial proposed solution we envisioned: a platform that would allow families to submit inquiries and receive quotes from multiple funeral homes in their local area. The families could choose the funeral home that worked best for them, and the funeral homes would only pay us a fee if the family chose to work with them. I got everything ready and hit "send" on the application – and exhaled.

Just a couple of weeks later, we received an email from the head of the program. The subject line: Congratulations, you've been selected to take part in the inaugural class of the 10xelerator.

Quitting our day jobs

Bryan and I were thrilled to get into the 10xelerator. We felt that it could expose us to networks that we simply didn't have, like Ohio's angel investor and venture capital community. The fact that the $20,000 they were contributing was through a grant that didn't have to be paid back was also nice. Getting into the 10xelerator program meant one uncomfortable reality, though: We would have to quit our jobs.

Bryan and I already agreed that getting into the 10xelerator would mark the leaping off point, but it didn't necessarily make it any easier. We had jobs – *good* jobs – that were finally beginning to reward us financially. Having to look the people in the eye who gave us an amazing opportunity and tell them that we were leaving would be tough. But we knew that they would understand. After all, *they* were entrepreneurs themselves.

On June 10th, 2011, Bryan and I each drove down to Columbus with a single suitcase and moved into a furnished guest house that Christopher and his wife, Nancy, had offered up to us. We got settled in, turned in relatively early, and went to bed knowing that the very next day would be day one for our business together.

1. ARE YOU SURE YOU NEED TO RAISE MONEY?

It's been said that time has surpassed money as the most precious commodity in existence today. It is out of respect of *your* time that I actually invite you to consider whether it's worth reading this book at all. If you've made the investment of time to actually begin reading, then it's probably likely that you're considering raising seed capital for your business. This book is meant to serve as a guide, of sorts, to help founders navigate the often-complicated process of finding the very first dollars of investment for their business.

But is this book really for you? There are a few important things to understand up front:

Raising capital doesn't guarantee success.

It's easy for first-time founders to view certain venture capitalists or entrepreneurs as icons. With A-listers such as Ashton Kutcher, Justin Beiber, and Lady Gaga making startup investments over the past several years along with funding rounds and acquisitions for companies like Facebook, Instagram, Snapchat, and others getting thrust into the nightly news spotlight, the line between investor and celebrity gets blurred even further.

With a renewed interest and recent spotlight shone brightly on the world of startups, many founders get carried away thinking more about which startup celebrity might write them their first investment check instead of how they will achieve product-market fit. No amount of startup capital *guarantees* success. Just a few years ago, Color Labs raised over $41 Million in initial funding from A-List investors and *still* managed to fail spectacularly, despite the great reputation and past successes of the company's founders.

You give away a little bit of yourself, and your company, with every investment dollar received.

It's not uncommon to hear the notion of "being one's own boss" as a primary reason for somebody to try their hand at becoming an entrepreneur. While it's true that running your own business could mean additional flexibility and freedom – the concept of a startup founder having no boss is a myth. In fact, instead of having one boss, startup founders have several.

For starters, even if you don't take a single cent of outside investment, your employees, co-founders, and customers are your primary bosses. You're essentially working for them. Even if these people report to you, you will (or at least, should) feel a sense of responsibility to them like you've never felt before. After all, these are the people who made sacrifices to join your team, work with you, and give your product a shot.

And now, you're considering bringing investors on board? Stuff is about to get real.

You don't just have an ethical responsibility to investors; you have a *fiduciary* responsibility as well. This means that you're legally obligated to act in the best interest of the owners of your company, which now includes outsiders. When you bring an investor on board, you give up the freedom you had when you owned 100% of the business.

The new shareholders in your company might have very different goals for the business than you had. A venture investor, for instance, generally strives to earn a 10x (or more!) return on an investment within 5-7 years. As such, they'll want to see their cash used to do everything possible to make that a reality. Taking their money doesn't mean that you can use it any way you see fit. Sure, the best investors will *tell* you that they're investing in you and that the strategic direction of the company is controlled by you. But, your vision better be in line with their vision, at least to the point where they can be somewhat confident that they'll see a return on their investment.

Bringing investors on board often means that the Founder will eventually be replaced with "professional" management. It's not uncommon for lead investors to end up with a seat (or two) on the Board of Directors of the company. This might as well be called the "Board of Bosses" because the CEO reports directly to this very Board. In fact, the Board of Directors even has the power to fire a CEO, and hire a new one, at their discretion. Great investors and great Boards can help a company immensely in many ways, from offering product/technology advice to helping find additional customers and investors. But don't underestimate the control that investors have over many aspects of the business.

Putting off investment can actually result in more value for founders.

All too often, the game plan for startup founders goes like this: Come up with a killer idea, assemble the best team to execute the idea, find money to fund the idea, build the company (or at minimum, an initial product) and try to gain customers. While the pieces of this plan make sense, the order is flawed. Even if it was possible to raise money before the product or business was built it may not actually be in the best interest of the founders.

Take the following scenario as an example:

A coffee-fueled night among three friends results in an idea for a startup venture. They decide that some funding could give their team a cushion as they build their product, so they leverage their network to take in $100,000 from an angel investor who believes in them and agree to give 20% of their startup in the form of equity in return. They then go on to build their product and sign up initial customers resulting in $100,000 in revenue. At this point, they decide to raise additional capital and receive an offer from a new investor to invest $1,000,000 in exchange for 40% of the company. Between the initial investment and new investment the founders retain 48% of the company, with their shares valued at $1.2M (on paper, of course).

On that same initial coffee-fueled night, another neighborhood café had patrons hatching a similar concept. They also have a strong network, but instead of seeking early investment funding at this stage, they decide to use their own "sweat equity," putting in more work themselves before taking on outside investment. They cobble together an initial product on their own, and find a way to sell it to customers. Before they knew it, they had also generated $100,000 in revenue. With this business traction, they decide to increase the momentum and raise a $1,000,000 investment round, in exchange for 40% of their business. After receiving the investment, the founders retain 60% of the company, with their shares valued at $1.5M (again, on paper).

Both groups were very similar. They had similar ideas, and had followed similar trajectories. Both even decided to raise money from investors *eventually*. However, the second group decided to get to revenue generation first before taking on investors. The first startup decided to raise $100,000 initially to pad their chances of success. While the difference in initial cash inflow is $100,000, the current value of the shares that the founders own in the first startup is $300,000 *less* than the value of the shares that the founders own in the second startup. A little sweat equity early on can pay off with a larger ownership percentage later.

For a side-by-side comparison of these two scenarios, visit: SeedFundingBook.com/FreeResources.

You may not be your local investors' type.

Investors like to invest in what they know. Over the past two decades, Silicon Valley has seen its share of successes in consumer Internet, enterprise software, B2B software-as-a-service, and other technology businesses. Millionaires and even Billionaires have been created as a result, and many of these successful entrepreneurs have become angel investors or venture capitalists and now invest in the next generation of entrepreneurs.

In other parts of the country like Cleveland and Detroit things are no different. However, those who invest in early stage businesses have seen their success come from different types of businesses. In Detroit, many angel investors have come from the auto industry. In Cleveland, there are many successful doctors and medical device professionals who have been willing to invest in medical-related businesses. In regions where software isn't in the DNA, it's harder for investors whose expertise and experience revolves around manufacturing or medical devices to invest in an iPhone app or B2B software platform. It's not to say that it can never happen, it's just not as likely.

I realize it's not fair to talk in absolutes. There are, of course, certain investors in almost any community who are willing to invest in a business that operates in a market they're not familiar with. There are also investors in places like Cleveland and Detroit that certainly do make investments in consumer Internet companies. However, it's important to note that the pool of investors inside and outside of Silicon Valley are quite different and also that every startup community has its own DNA that makes it unique.

The Big Takeaway

In short, raising one million dollars, or anything at all, might not even matter. What matters is whether or not you have a *viable business* on your hands. If you don't, all of the money in the world might not help you in the long run.

How can you determine if your startup idea actually has the potential to develop into a real business even though you're in the beginning, exploratory stages? Instead of focusing time and effort on raising seed capital, you may be better off focusing your time on proving out your business model. You may not be able to prove everything out initially; you could break your business model down into smaller, bite-size experiments and test them one-by-one. If you can prove that the business can grow organically before you need to take in seed capital, then you may not even need to take in money to validate your business.

An Investor's Perspective
Robert Hatta, Drive Capital

Ask any young startup about their biggest challenges at any given moment, and just behind attracting money is attracting talent. Robert Hatta helps solve that problem for startups as the Talent Partner for

Drive Capital, one of the largest early-stage venture capital funds outside of New York and California. In his role, he works with portfolio companies to formulate strategies to find, recruit, and retain the best talent possible. Robert also works with entrepreneurs at the earliest of stages – attending hackathons, demo days, and other events where young founders gather. As active as Robert is, talent-related observations aren't the only ones he makes."

"It's easy for founders to get caught up in the allure of fundraising. Entrepreneurs should remember that raising capital isn't the ultimate destination. It's simply one form of fuel to help get you there. Raising seed capital can be stressful – especially when you're trying to build your business at the same time. However, closing a round of funding doesn't really deserve much celebration. True entrepreneurs know that this is the time to roll up their sleeves and focus on building the business into the successful venture it was intended to be, as *that's* the destination they're trying to reach."

Robert gives some hope for young founders who find themselves outside of one of the more established tech startup communities like Silicon Valley.

"Founders don't have to be in Silicon Valley to get their first million dollars in seed capital. The truth is that it can be done anywhere. The terms might be different based on your location, and it might take some time. But most markets have enough angel and seed investors to get a good idea and competent team off the ground, so long as their idea is truly big."

2. THE ONLY CHAPTER YOU MAY NEED TO READ

Traction: It's what investors everywhere are looking for in order to determine whether to anoint your startup "the next big thing" and inject the cold, hard cash needed to accelerate your business. If you can't find traction, forget raising capital -- your business will struggle just to stay alive. Find traction, and raising capital will never be an issue for you. It's important, however, to understand what traction *really* is and what it isn't.

Traction is not about raising capital.

Your ability to get a dollar of investment from one investor and two dollars from another investor the very next day gives you investment momentum, but it does not give you real business *traction*. Convincing investors to give you money does not get you any closer to determining whether or not you have a business on your hands. The only thing it proves is that you have the ability to convince investors to give you money.

Traction is not getting a press hit from Mashable or Huffington Post.

Media coverage can be nice. It can result in spikes in traffic and can serve as a nice marketing piece to send to a potential customer when pitching your business. But media coverage is not traction. It's not a growth engine that your business can rely upon. After all, the traffic that an article brings may not be the kind of traffic you want.

Traction isn't even necessarily about getting users or generating revenue.

Not all users or customer dollars are created equal. You start off having a very specific plan for building your business. If that plan includes selling $99 monthly memberships for your software-as-a-service business – and instead you convince a customer to pay you $250,000 to do a custom software development project – not one dollar of that quarter million is proof that your core "engine of growth" will actually work (unless, of course, your business model included offering custom software development work). It doesn't mean that you shouldn't take on that custom software project. In fact, a project like that could help fund your business. Just don't mistake it as traction for your core business.

Traction is what separates a viable business from a really good idea. It's what shows that your business can grow and sustain itself. It's a way to show that a dollar invested into your business will always result in three dollars of revenue. It's the proof that your business model isn't based on assumptions, but on actual hard data.

Most startups, especially at the stage where they're seeking seed capital, don't have true traction. They may have a great idea, solid team, and good plan, but they rarely have any demonstrable proof that they have an actual business on their hands. Fundraising can be a struggle for these teams, especially *outside* of Silicon Valley, where the risk tolerance of investors tends to be much lower. The more that startups can prove that they actually have a viable business, the better chance they'll have of securing seed capital.

But you're a startup. How are you supposed to get traction at this stage?

You feel like you need funding to get your business started – yet in order to get funding, you have to be able to show that you have a real business to invest in. What's a startup founder to do?

In order to get to a point where you can show startup traction, consider taking the following steps.

Build a prototype

The reality is that most investors – whether they're inside or outside of Silicon Valley – don't invest in ideas. They invest in businesses (or, at least projects that look like they have the potential to become businesses one day). At the earliest stages, it might be very difficult to illustrate to investors how your idea can actually be a business. So show them by building a prototype. Let them see, touch, and feel what your product will actually look like. The more functional your prototype is, the better. Mockups, a video demo, or even a more limited splash page can potentially serve as feasible prototypes for digital products. For physical products, illustrations or 3D printed prototypes are both cost-effective approaches that a founder can take in order to get to the prototype stage.

Get your customers in line.

Don't have a fully finished product yet? Don't worry. You can start to queue up your users and customers now rather than wait until you launch. Products like LaunchRock allow you to create a customizable landing page that describes your business, and starts collecting information from people who might be interested in learning more when you're ready to launch. Before you ever write a single line of code, you can market your product and begin to effectively build demand. Drew Houston, CEO of DropBox, famously launched a landing page and video for his now uber-popular file sharing service. DropBox's main product, while now a mainstream tool that many rely on, didn't even exist at the time Houston released this video. It didn't matter. Houston designed his landing page to show what the service could look like when it did finally exist. After the video was live, Houston shared it with people in networks like HackerNews and began to build an audience. This initial marketing effort resulted in tens of thousands of potential users signing up to use the product when it launched.

Start selling to customers before you even have a product.

Most new products ultimately see the traditional "lifecycle" of various types of customers – beginning with Innovators and Early Adopters. These two groups of customers are very open to using new technologies and products so long as it solves a significant problem or is extremely novel. If your solution can solve a specific problem for a targeted user group, they may very well be willing to pay you for it, even if it doesn't exist yet. For these customer types, consider making a special offer. Allow them to provide feedback during the development process and have a role in shaping the final product; when completed, they will be among the first to receive it. In exchange, they should agree to pay for the product, perhaps even putting a small deposit down early on. For customers who are hesitant to agree to pay for something that doesn't yet exist, you may consider making a non-binding offer. In this case, they won't be contractually obligated to become a customer but if they're involved in the development process (and especially if they paid a small deposit), they'll be psychologically invested regardless of what their formal contract with you says.

The Big Takeaway

Startups shouldn't be in the business of raising money; they should be in the business of delivering value to customers. While it can be daunting to demonstrate traction during the earliest stage of a startup, remember that something is better than nothing. Find a way to show traction, even if it's minimal. This way you'll appear more fundable to investors than startup founders who are simply talking about ideas. More importantly, this traction can help serve as validation for *you* and help determine whether or not to continue investing your valuable time and resources.

An Investor's Perspective
David Cohen, Techstars

David Cohen has seen more than his fair share of startup pitches, perhaps more than anybody else outside of Silicon Valley. As the Founder, Managing Partner, and CEO of Techstars – a mentorship-driven, seed stage investment accelerator with programs throughout the country, David has overseen investments made in over 400 companies that have collectively gone on to raise over $800M in capital. Techstars Ventures has also invested in dozens of startups, including popular companies such as Uber, Twilio, and SendGrid.

David understands the challenge that many startup founders are faced with when they're just getting off of the ground: they have an idea that may require some funding, but without that funding it's difficult to prove that their concept can translate into a viable business. David challenges founders to take another step.

"Assuming that there's an awesome team in place, I need to at least see a prototype in order to consider investing. I prefer to actually get to use the product, even if it's just an early, functional version. But a prototype, at minimum, shows me that the team knows how to create *something*."

Of course, the "if you build it, they will come" mantra typically doesn't work for most startups. Investors generally want to know whether a product will actually resonate with customers. David considers this as well when evaluating a startup.

"A functional product alone isn't enough. I'm always curious about whether customers or users will find the product to be useful. It might be tough to prove this in the early stages, but it's not impossible. A consumer-oriented business can promote their concept and begin to attract early sign-ups very early on, before their product is even built. Business-to-business enterprises can show traction by asking potential customers to sign a Letter of Intent. In either case, when a startup is able to show me that customers are actually interested in the solution that they have to offer – even before their product is fully built and launched – I take notice."

With all of the success that David has had as an investor, people might think that they have to have an Ivy League degree or Silicon Valley pedigree to catch his interest. They'd be wrong, though.

"People are people, and great founders are great founders – no matter where they live. I'm proud of the founders that I've invested in who reside throughout the United States, and even abroad."

Interested in adding David as an investor? Just visit Techstars.com. With its eight distinct programs scattered throughout the United States and the handful of other accelerators "powered by Techstars", there's almost always a Techstars class accepting applications.

3. UNDERSTAND YOUR WHY

Startups are used to describing their "what." It doesn't take very long to sit through a bad pitch competition to be inundated by the monotonous and uninspiring ways that many startups describe themselves. The pitches that cause everyone's eyes to gloss over and start reaching for their smartphone usually focus on the "what" of what their startup does:

Example #1: "We are a local-social-mobile platform that helps small businesses engage with their customers…"

Example #2: "We are an online community that caters to the $20 Billion tax professional market…"

Example #3: "Our novel tool integrates with our customer's CRM platform to capture user-specific data…"

See what I mean? I bet you're already reaching for that smartphone right now to swipe yourself away from this pain. Yet, it's not like the one-liners above aren't *descriptive*. They are. But the problem is that they don't evoke a deeper meaning. They don't have any emotional pull.

We struggled with this at eFuneral, at first. We were passionate about what we were doing and our business had very real meaning to us. But when we tried to describe it to investors, customers, and partners – it didn't show through at first.

"We're an online platform that connects families in need with the funeral homes that can best serve them."

That was our original one-liner for eFuneral. And it was horrible. Sure it described *what* we did. But really, nobody cared about that part. It didn't evoke any sort of visceral reaction. At best, and only because we operated within an industry that is so foreign to most, it may have raised some eyebrows and opened up the door for us to explain a bit more. In general, though, it was a statement that lacked meaning and purpose.

So we tried again:

"We help families get the information they need to make more informed funeral decisions."

This was the next way that we described eFuneral and it was a little bit closer to our "why". The statement itself infers that families currently don't have the information that is needed to make informed funeral decisions, and we are the group that can provide them that information. Yet it was still more of a "what" than a "why". But when we started to talk about eFuneral this way, more people started to listen to us. Investors, especially, began to ask questions. They were curious about the information that families currently didn't have access to, and how we were planning on providing it to them (and, of course, monetizing as a result).

"We're bringing transparency to an industry that desperately needs it – funeral planning.

Aha! It clicked. *That's* a "why" – or at least a giant step in the right direction. Does it actually describe what it is that we do? No – but it didn't matter, because we learned that our "what" could be described later. When we led with our "why", people actually wanted to continue to engage with us and dig deeper. Conceptually, they understood that the funeral planning process was archaic and confusing – and many had the first-hand experience to prove it. They believed that the lack of transparency needed to change for consumers, and understood that our mission was to change it. Now that they knew our "why", we could have the conversation about the "what" because they actually cared.

Specifically for investors, the "why" matters for a few reasons:

It shows that there's a problem to be solved.

It's true that many of the best products are actually solutions to problems that people experience. When the "why" of a startup resonates with an investor, the investor is already sold on the fact that there is a problem to be solved. Getting the investor to believe in the problem you're solving is half the battle in winning over investors. In fact, it may even be more than half of the battle. Even the most successful companies have solutions that change and evolve over time. Investors understand this, and know that their role is helping startups as they navigate the evolution of their solution. Yet, while these solutions evolve – the problem they're solving for often remains the same.

Investors need to know that you're in this for the long haul.

What keeps startup founders motivated after they've lost a key customer? What encourages a startup team when they're running on little to no cash? How is a founder expected to push forward when she keeps running into technical challenges? Is it the reminder that their company is meant to be a "social platform catering to the XYZ industry?" Definitely not. Is it their desire to become billionaires when their company goes public? While this might be a rosy dream that founders have when they first get started, this is usually not the carrot that keeps founders pushing forward when the going gets tough. Startup teams persevere because they are completely and unequivocally dedicated to solving the big problem they set out to solve. They stay motivated because of the "why".

Investors know that customers (and employees) will care about the "why."

Investors aren't going to invest in a business solely because of a startup's "why". It's true that they want to see that there can be an actual business that can be built to solve the big problem and that there's an accomplished team that's behind the solution. However, investors know that the "why" is what resonates with customers and employees. Even outside of Silicon Valley, the job market for startup-ready talent can be brutal. How is a startup supposed to compete with the other, hotter startups in the area for the best technical talent? How is a startup with no track record supposed to sell to its first client? Clearly communicating and owning your "why" is one way to set your startup apart from all of the others. It's what employees and customers can buy into.

The Big Takeaway

It's important to articulate what your startup does. But describing the "what" is not enough to win over investors. Instead, articulating and owning the "why" that drives your startup will allow investors to relate more easily, and help them buy into the fact that you're solving a problem that deserves to be solved.

Still need more ideas on how to define and articulate your startup's "why"? Check out the book "Start with Why" by Simon Sinek.

An Entrepreneur's Perspective
Blake Squires, Movable

Blake Squires is one of those entrepreneurs with the "Midas Touch." Whatever project he gets involved in seems to turn into gold. His first two startup ventures – Everstream (where he was an early member of the management team) and Findaway (where he was a co-founder) – both turned into high-growth, multi-million dollar revenue producing companies. After his time at Findaway, he started thinking about his next move. With the successes that he already had, his options were certainly open. The chances were high that he could accept an executive role with local area tech company or hang out his own shingle as a consultant. As a true entrepreneur, however, Blake knew that his next move would be to another startup – one where he was the founder and idea guy. He began to seriously think about the kind of startup he wanted to focus on.

"There was this defining moment for me when I was hanging out at home one evening with my wife, who was reading a magazine. I remember turning to her and asking, 'If we could do *anything*, what's next? Give me an idea that I can be passionate about'. Glancing down at the magazine she was reading, a startling statistic stood out. One in three kids in the United States are considered obese, with the numbers only increasing. The light bulb went off for us at that moment, and it became clear that we had to do something, *anything* to get kids moving. We decided to embark on a mission to help children live healthier lives."

Blake's new venture, Movable, is indeed getting people moving. Thousands of schools, employers, and other entities have signed up to incorporate the wearable Movband device and online platform into their suite of employee benefits. While Blake is encouraged and excited to see his business grow, he's most proud of Movable's mission-driven focus.

"Somebody recently asked me when I knew I wanted to become a social entrepreneur, and I had to stop and really consider whether I actually was one. But admittedly, at this point in my life, I care not only about starting and growing a business but also making a difference in the world. My previous businesses created a lot of value, and I'm proud of them. But Movable is making a real difference every day and *that's* what drives me."

Aside from being a successful entrepreneur, Blake also has some experience as an investor as Principal in Hatch Partners, a seed fund that was an early investor in eFuneral. As an investor, Blake actively looks for the entrepreneur to have passion around what they're creating. He always seeks to understand the "why" and the spark behind the founder's motivation.

"I can tell the difference between those founders who truly have passion and those who are just going through the motions. I've always been more interested in the founders who show real passion for what it is that they're doing. Everybody can have a great idea. But fewer people have the credibility and experience to turn that idea into a business. And even fewer people have real *passion* to turn that business into something special. Those are the people who I want to work with."

4. KNOW YOUR NUMBERS

Whether you're raising money from investors or not, it's absolutely critical that you have a firm understanding of how your startup will use cash, and how spending that money will generate growth for your business. This doesn't mean that you have to have fully-baked three year financial plan. Most seed-stage investors won't ask for this. You also don't need to have a former corporate CFO on your team or be a group of quantitative ninjas who can spew out statistical analyses on the fly. In fact, hiring a CFO or pure "numbers guy" is probably a terrible first hire, as your initial team should be focused on building and selling your product. What's most important is that founders have an understanding of the market opportunity and how they can expend resources to better leverage their market opportunity.

There are some common "Red Flags" that investors look for when founders present their financial models and revenue forecasts. To investors, these "Red Flags" are often signs of immaturity, inexperience, or – worse – a lack of integrity:

Red Flag #1: "If we can get just 10% of the market..."

Yes, it's true that if you can get "just 10%" of a $10 Billion market your company will be the next billion-dollar company. You might then take your company public, appear on the covers of Fast Company and Fortune, and become the talk of the town. There's just one problem. You have to actually *get* to that point. Saying that you only have to achieve 10% (or 1%, or even .1%) of a particular market is what's called the "Top Down" approach, and it shows that you might be naïve in the ways of business. Instead, it's important to work from the bottom up. What does one sale look like for your company? How much did it cost you to achieve that one sale? How did you scale that one sale to turn into many sales? This is what investors care about.

Red Flag #2: "Our conservative estimates are..."

Everybody's "conservative" when they're presenting their revenue forecasts to investors. In reality, typical "conservative" revenue forecasts are usually quite the opposite. They're bloated with assumptions, and include targets that will never get hit. This alone isn't a major issue with investors, as they realize that startup founders aren't fortune-tellers. However, they appreciate honesty over bravado when explaining a financial model. What are the major assumptions that you're making? What are the inherent risks? It's better to be up front and transparent with investors when it comes to revenue drivers and expenses.

Red Flag #3: "There's no need for a marketing budget since our product will go viral..."

Investors love products that are truly viral. But "going viral" isn't something you can just bank on. Even if you made a painstaking effort to design the product you're launching to be inherently viral, you're likely going to need to, at minimum, give your customers a nudge in the beginning. More likely, you're going to need to market your product quite a bit in some way. This doesn't mean that you have to spend lots of money on a Super Bowl commercial. There are creative ways to get your product in front of customers. The point is that investors want to see that you've given serious thought to how your customers will learn about and purchase your product, and you had better be prepared to share this thinking with them. Even better is if you can actually show investors how your product is leveraging real network effects to grow your customer base.

Red Flag #4: "We'll need to spend about $10 Million in advertising before we generate revenue..."

This mistake is on the opposite end of the spectrum of Red Flag #3. The problem here is assuming that you will need to spend massive amounts of money before you're going to earn a dime. To be clear, there are many investors that are perfectly okay with startups that don't plan to monetize initially. Be aware that these investors are much less common outside of New York and Silicon Valley than inside.

However, most investors are still wary of those startups that want to raise significant funding for the primary purposes of marketing, as a $1 million marketing campaign has a chance to be completely wasted money. What's important to investors is your ability to articulate how money spent on marketing will result in additional value for your company, whether that value is in the form of revenue, or any other metric that is important to your startup.

Red Flag #5: "Sales will increase by exactly 300% in year 1 and exactly 200% in year 2…"

Statements like this show that you simply haven't given enough thought to your numbers. It could be true that your startup ultimately achieves these goals. But overly round numbers like 100% and 50% make it obvious that you chose these numbers out of the blue and are using the "Top Down" approach when making your estimates. It's less important what the numbers actually are. What's important is that you actually know why these numbers belong in your financial model and forecast.

It's important to avoid these red flags, but it's also critical to allow investors see that you actually *do* know what you're talking about when it comes to your financial model. Investors' expectations can vary at the startup seed stage. Government-backed programs that offer funding to startups, whether it's as a loan or direct investment, can sometimes require a fully baked 5-year Profit and Liability forecast. Accelerators, Venture Capital, and Angel Investors usually don't require a 5-year P&L – however, they will still have very pointed questions about your financial model.

No matter what type of funding sources you plan on targeting, before you spend your entire weekend in front of the computer crunching away in Excel, pause for a moment and realize that your effort should first be spent on what's most important. A single page spreadsheet that outlines your startup's most critical assumptions on how you will generate revenue, and how you will have to spend money in order to generate that revenue, is the best place to start. It's important to tie these fields together with logic so that when one assumption is changed, the other fields adjust accordingly. Building these assumptions out using the "Bottom Up" approach is truly the most thoughtful way of building out a financial model. While it might take time to get the data you need to formulate your assumptions, once you have this information, you can create a 5-year P&L forecast in less time than you'd think. But you have to know those assumptions first.

Separately, be sure to be well versed on the financial models of similar businesses that have achieved scale. These businesses don't necessarily have to be direct competitors but should be analogous to the business that you're growing.

Let's focus on one of the important assumptions that eFuneral made: our Total Market Size. This was difficult to articulate, as the funeral Internet marketing space wasn't exactly a hot market that everybody talked about, and therefore clear-cut data was hard to find. Ultimately, we were able to determine that our Total Market Size (Death Care Marketing) was $923.51 Million.

Notice that $923.51 Million isn't a nice round number like $950 Million or even $1 Billion. It's a very specific number that we were able to derive based off of the following data points and assumptions we made:

Total U.S. Population: 311,401,703

Annual U.S. Death Rate at the time: .0083

Average Cost of a Burial Service: $7,755

% of Deaths resulting in a Burial Service: 63.14%

Average Cost of a Cremation: $1,600

% of Deaths resulting in a Cremation: 36.86%

% of a funeral home's marketing budget: 5.5%

Some of the information above was available through the United States Census, such as the Population and Death Rate figures. Other information, such as the Average Burial and Cremation Costs, were derived from industry reports we were able to find. Estimating a funeral home's marketing budget required a little more heavy lifting. This was an assumption that we made based off of interviews we conducted with a dozen funeral homes. Regardless, we were able to speak confidently about our market size, and if an investor tried to question our numbers, we were able to back our figures up with real data and educated assumptions. Even when an investor disagreed with our estimates, we earned their respect by the way that we derived this figure.

David Teten and Paul Bianco, venture capitalists at ff Venture Capital in New York City, offer great examples of startup financial models along with other helpful resources for startup founders. Direct links to the resources from both David and Paul can be found at SeedFundingBook.com/FreeResources.

The Big Takeaway

While you don't have to be a quantitative genius, it's critical that you understand the key components of how your business will actually work. Remember that it's OK to make assumptions about your business model, however, you should be prepared to talk about why those assumptions were made and what effect it will have on your financial plan if those assumptions are wrong.

An Investor's Perspective
Blair Garrou, Mercury Fund

Blair Garrou isn't a Silicon Valley veteran, and he's OK with that. In fact, he embraces it. As a successful entrepreneur-turned-venture capitalist, Blair makes his living investing in companies *outside* of Silicon Valley. His role as a mentor to various accelerators located in different parts of the country such as The Brandery, Techstars, and SURGE further prove his dedication for finding and funding startups in places that others might not pay attention to.

For business-minded entrepreneurs who plan on wowing Blair with a fully built out 5-year financial plan, don't be surprised if Blair isn't impressed.

"One of the biggest mistakes I see entrepreneurs make when they're pitching at the seed stage is focusing *too much* on the financial plan. I don't want to see a fully-baked financial plan that spans several years. It's all a guess at this point. Instead, entrepreneurs should focus on the basic economic model: What is the total addressable market? What are comparable products in the marketplace, and how are they priced? How will the product be sold – and what does it cost to sell the product? These are the questions I'm looking for entrepreneurs to have good answers for at the seed stage."

But, what if an entrepreneur doesn't have all of the answers? What if the entrepreneur's economic model is built on a few major assumptions?

"I'm most attracted to founders who are resourceful and self-taught. Rather than showing me numbers based on a lot of guesses, I'm interested in the experiments that founders have run to test those assumptions. I want people to come to me and say, 'Here's what we thought. Here's a test we ran to prove it out – and here's what we learned. What do you think?' These interactions often turn into more in-depth and meaningful conversations down the road ."

Of course, in the end it won't be the numbers alone that will impress Blair. To him, investing isn't simply a financial-driven decision.

"Entrepreneurs should realize that taking an investment from a venture capitalist isn't just about accepting money. You're entering into a *relationship* that you'll be in for the next 5-10 years. Yes, I expect entrepreneurs to know their fundamental business model, but I don't just invest in the numbers. I like to get to know entrepreneurs really well before investing. In fact, if people are coming to me for the first time when they actually need money – they're probably too late. Most of the entrepreneurs I've invested in have been people who I've gotten to know over the course of several months. They've come to me and have asked for feedback. By the time I make the decision to invest, I know them very well."

5. EMBRACE BEING A BIG FISH

As soon you step out of your car and onto University Avenue in Palo Alto, California, the home of Stanford University and the center of Silicon Valley, you realize pretty quickly that you're in the land of startup opportunity. On one short walk, you'll pass by world-class software developers and web designers grabbing coffee, you'll walk past the headquarters of the product design titan, IDEO, and you will pass by offices of the companies behind many of the software applications loaded onto the smartphone in your pocket.

You'll also realize that it's a pretty crowded land. In your visit to Palo Alto, Mountain View, or even San Francisco you'll notice just how many other startup founders are fighting for attention from the same group of investors, mentors, and media outlets.

Silicon Valley is the epicenter of tech startups and the venture capital firms that fund them. However, nearly every major metropolitan market has a startup community. Certain markets such as New York, Los Angeles, Boulder, and Austin have startup communities that are thriving and flourishing. Other smaller startup communities, such as those in rust belt cities like Cleveland, Pittsburgh, and Detroit have just begun to develop.

There are many factors that lead to the development of the most successful startup communities, including a combination of talent, direct investment, and a track record for major entrepreneurial successes. However, it can take quite some time for a community to experience major wins or for investors to change their behavior and begin to consider investing in startups versus later-stage investments.

Regardless of whether you find yourself in a nascent or established startup community it's important to understand that you have an opportunity to place yourself squarely in the center of whatever community you're in. Particularly in the smaller communities with less developed entrepreneurial ecosystems, you have an opportunity to step up and establish yourself as a leader (which is precisely what many investors look for).

Most investors in startups say that the team is the most important piece of the puzzle. It's not just technical aptitude that investors are interested in, but also its leadership. How is the founder going to convince others to join the team and compete against bigger, more established companies? How is the founder going to convince customers to give their startup company a shot over entrenched competitors? Being a leader within your own startup community is one way to showcase your talents to the very investors who can ultimately fund your company.

How can you position yourself as a leader within your own startup community?

Make coffee dates.

Before you can lead within your own startup community, you have to actually know the players. Who are the founders of some of the more promising startups? Who are the current thought leaders on the subject? Who is putting on events that draw startup founders and investors? You can start to get to know these people right now by simply identifying them and asking them to meet over coffee. Make sure that there's a purpose to the meeting beyond simply meeting them; whether it's asking for feedback on a topic that they're an expert on, or offering them help in an area where they might need some assistance. It's true that everybody has a busy life – particularly those active within startup communities. But it's important to find a way to get to know the people actively involved in your startup community on a personal level.

Add value to others.

Once you get to know others who are in your startup community, make it a point to add value. Are you an SEO expert? Offer to help mentor other startups that need help in this specific area. Do you know about a startup seeking funding whose business model meets the investment criteria of an investor with whom you're familiar? Ask the investor if they'd be willing to meet with the founder. In a thriving startup community – people trade on a currency of reciprocity. What goes around actually does come around. This doesn't happen by accident, though. It happens because you've established your reputation as a founder who helps others and when the time comes when *you* need help, you'll be quick to get it.

Provide opportunities to congregate and connect.

One of the many reasons that Silicon Valley can be a great place to launch a startup is all of the opportunities for serendipity. It's not uncommon to hear stories about a founder meeting a potential investor while at a café, or for a key team position to be filled because of a chance meeting at a hackathon. Outside of Silicon Valley these chance encounters happen less, primarily because there are just fewer opportunities. Use this as an opportunity to step in and fill the void. Do you have an idea for a great technology event that would serve your startup community well? Begin to plan it. If that sounds too daunting, you can start smaller. Consider planning a "startup meet-up" where the various startups within your community can meet for a few beers at a local bar or café. Launch a private Facebook group that is open only to those who are active within your startup community. By creating ways for your startup community to congregate, you're also putting yourself squarely in the center without even realizing it.

A word of caution:

While we were in the beginning stages of building eFuneral, I admittedly wasn't *trying* to be "the connector." I didn't invite others to coffee in an effort to become a startup community leader. I didn't offer to help others with the hope that they would "pay me back" later on. I got to know and helped others because I was genuinely interested in building relationships with other startup founders and I enjoyed helping out when I could. I just think entrepreneurs are really interesting people. I fully believe that this authentic approach is what helped me establish myself as a leader within Cleveland's startup community. Keep this notion of authenticity in mind, as your efforts may be wasted if you're only doing it to check off some boxes in your grandmaster plan. If you actually care about getting to know and helping others in your startup community it will show and your generosity will be recognized and rewarded.

The Big Takeaway

Rather than focus on the disadvantages that your startup may have by being located outside of Silicon Valley, embrace the advantages that exist instead. You have an opportunity to be a leader within your own startup community, and building this skill set can be quite rewarding.

An Entrepreneur's Perspective
Brian Trautschold, Ambition

Like many other stories about a promising startup's founding team, the story of Travis, Brian, Wes, and Jared starts in the confines of a college dorm room where they constantly bounced ideas off of each other in-between classes, midterm exams, and other activities that typically keep college students busy. The major difference between this story and some others like it is that the college campus wasn't Stanford, UC Berkeley, Harvard, or any other Ivy League (or Ivy League-esque) school. These guys all went to the University of Tennessee, a university that certainly has a fine academic program, but may be better known for being home to Peyton Manning than for being a hotbed of future technology startups.

After college, Brian found himself in Little Rock, Arkansas working for tech giant, HP. Just about a year later, Brian packed up his car and drove a few hours east to follow his future wife to Chattanooga. Within just a few months, Travis and another friend, Jared, left the ski-bum lifestyle they had been enjoying in Lake Tahoe to join Brian in Chattanooga. They all began to integrate themselves into the small, but nascent, startup community there, and continued searching for that billion-dollar startup idea. The ideas ranged but typically centered on the explosive growth of the Internet.

Brian recalled the process of moving to Chattanooga and getting entrenched into the startup community there. "When we moved to Chattanooga, there were really only two or three other internet startups around. There didn't seem to be very many people serving as active investors and mentors to the Internet companies that did exist. Then, we met this awesome group of people now known as The Lamp Post Group who had successfully built and exited companies together, and who were also passionate about technology. We were lucky enough for them to take us under their wing a bit. They told us that they weren't sure about some of the ideas that we had at the time, but they still wanted to invest in *us*. They wrote the first investment check we ever received. We happened to be in the right place, at the right time – and met the right group of people.

A few years later, the foursome was accepted into the Y-Combinator accelerator in Silicon Valley, which is regarded as the most elite accelerator in the world having spawned successful titans like DropBox, AirBnB, and others. Their new company, Ambition, a motivation and analytics platform for sales teams, was ultimately voted by other Y-Combinator companies as one of the most promising startups of their class. Yet, despite winning the respect of their peers, investors, and others within Silicon Valley, when the three-month program was over, the team decided to pack up and move back to Chattanooga to launch their business. Brian reflects upon that decision.

"The density of startup and investors in Silicon Valley is undeniable, and there are benefits to being there. But ultimately, we wanted to get to work. We felt that the best place to do that was back in Chattanooga, away from the distractions that Silicon Valley can sometimes bring. And we're happy with the decision we made. In Chattanooga, we've made a name for ourselves here as offering one of the best companies in town for those who want to work in a fast-paced startup culture. We've been able to tap into an awesome network of regional universities for top-notch talent."

On the notion of whether a startup has to be in Silicon Valley to succeed, Brian sums up their belief by pointing to their growing customer base.

"It's true that investors in Silicon Valley can pressure you to base your company near where the investor lives and works. But at the end of the day, we're a business that serves our customers. And we've never lost one customer because of the fact that our company isn't headquartered in San Francisco or Palo Alto."

6. BUILD A MILLION DOLLAR TEAM

If you ask ten investors what they're looking for in a startup, you will get a number of different answers. The one constant, however, is their desire to invest in a strong startup team. This fact can seem counter-intuitive to many first time startup founders. They tend to assume that the idea is the most important thing when pitching to investors. It's true that a novel idea might catch an investor's attention, but as Thomas Edison said, "the value of an idea is in the use of it." Indeed, it is the execution of ideas that typically separates startups that last from those that don't. Sophisticated investors understand this, which is why they invest in companies that have teams who can properly execute, no matter how unique (or not) the business idea might be.

Chances are that, if you're reading this, you have already begun to build your team, or perhaps you're early on in the idea stage where you'll soon begin looking for team members. No matter what stage you're in, it's important to know that there are specific steps that you can take as it relates to building your team that will improve your chances of getting funded:

Make sure your team shares the mission, not ideas.

It's easy for new startups to fall prey to what I call "Mirror Syndrome" when building out their initial startup team. If your team of co-founders looks and acts exactly like you, you've already fallen victim. With "Mirror Syndrome", the skill-set, strengths, and even the background of the team all looks the same. This is actually not too surprising, as many startups start with a duo or trio who meet over a beer or during a coffee fueled evening of discussion. Yet, because people naturally gravitate towards others who share common interests and, generally, are similar to them, this group of friends is probably composed of like-minded people. This can be great for a circle of friends, but surrounding yourself with people similar to you can be a fatal mistake in a startup. Instead, founders should build out their initial team with individuals whose backgrounds and skill sets are diverse and complimentary.

Aside from skill set, the ideal startup team should reflect diversity in other ways as well.

Level of experience

Can three recent college dropouts really relate to what a 1,000 employee organization deals with on a daily basis in order to create an enterprise software product that meets their needs? It's possible, but it's more likely that having somebody on the startup team that has had some enterprise-level experience could offer much needed perspective.

Gender / Ethnic Background

Are you building a product that only white men will use? Even if the answer is unequivocally yes, I'll argue that having a startup team made up of only white men would be a big mistake. A team with a diverse background lessens the chance of groupthink prevailing and forces a team to think about different approaches to solving problems and thinking critically.

While a startup should have a team that's diverse in skill sets, background, and ways of thinking, it's critical that the "why" fueling the startup's creation is bought into by every team member. We already discussed the importance of having a "why," but this singular mission of the startup should be the driving force behind the culture. Every step that the startup takes, from individual contributions to major team efforts, should be taken to accomplish the greater mission of the organization. Remember, it's more than okay for people to think differently and challenge each other as long as everybody agrees on the overall "why," the reason that the startup exists in the first place.

Do I need partners?

In any startup, founders wear many hats. For solo entrepreneurs, it can be pretty daunting to face all of the challenges a startup presents alone. This is one reason that startup teams with multiple co-founders are generally more common than startups with solo founders, particularly when it comes to companies seeking funding from angel or venture capital investors. Regardless, whether you have a startup team made up of one or five, each team member should accept that they'll need to function as a generalist in the early days of the organization's existence. This doesn't mean that they can't have a specialty area, just that everyone needs to be flexible in order to get all the necessary tasks accomplished.

Quite often, non-technical founders ask me how they can find a technical counterpart. And then, when they realize how difficult it is to find one (truth be told, finding the right one is like finding a needle in a haystack), their next question is whether or not they should simply outsource the development of the technology to an IT job shop or independent freelancers. There isn't a simple answer to the question of outsource vs. develop in-house. However, as a rule of thumb, if the core of what you're doing is technology based, investors generally want to see that technology is engrained within the team itself. If the core of what you're doing *isn't* really technology dependent, it may be best to focus your startup team-building efforts elsewhere. In the latter scenario, you and your partner can implement the technical components using off-the-shelf platforms like Wordpress, Shopify and Stripe, or you can find an independent contractor to help you get up and running. It's not to say that having a technical co-founder couldn't be helpful in this situation but it may not be absolutely necessary in order to get funded.

When building your startup team, ask yourself this question: What skill sets, knowledge base, and expertise is needed in order to get to the point where you can prove you are on the trajectory of growth for your business? If you already possess all of these traits yourself, you may have a legitimate shot at getting funded as a solo entrepreneur. More than likely, however, there are going to be holes that exist once you've done this inventory process. Building your startup team should be about filling these holes.

Treat your partners like you would a spouse.

Having a partner in a startup is similar to having a partner in a domestic relationship. You'll spend countless hours with this person, often times, more. You'll have major ups and major downs. You'll rely on this person to prop you up when you're feeling defeated, and you'll be their champion when they need you to be. In short, your professional lives will be reliant on one another with your success being directly tied to their success. It's serious stuff.

Because it's so serious, treat relationships that you have with co-founders as such. Ask yourself these questions to quickly test whether you're taking startup co-founders as seriously as you should:

Would you ever propose marriage to somebody that you just met an hour ago at a speed-dating event? If the answer is no, then don't even considering partnering with somebody immediately after meeting them at a founder-dating event or online matching service. Get to know them for a while first.

Would you consider asking somebody at the beginning of a first date if they'd be open to marrying you? If not, then don't ask this question to potential co-founders when meeting them for the first time. Dig in and understand more about them before you decide whether you want them on your founding team.

Would you marry somebody without knowing anything about his or her parents or immediate family? If you wouldn't, then why would you not try to know more about a potential co-founder's personal situation? You may be open to working 100-hour weeks and eating/living/breathing your startup. However, if your potential co-founder has a young family and wishes to work more reasonable hours, you'll be launching your startup on the wrong foot by not being aligned with each other from the start.

Investors will be the first to point out that many startups fail because of major issues and differences between the founders. And it's true that divorce does, unfortunately, happen – even with founders. Have a very open and candid conversation with your potential co-founder(s) so you can do your best to avoid a bad breakup down the road.

Be all in

There's a saying that startup founders must have "skin in the game" in order to even get consideration from investors. Some people mistake this to mean that you have to put a second mortgage on your home, invest your entire life savings into your startup, and put you and your family at serious financial risk. You don't. In fact, you *shouldn't*. Investors understand that everybody's personal financial situation is unique and can usually accept that your version of being "all in" might be different from somebody else's. But it is true that they need to know that you're 100% committed to your startup.

What this means is that you're not likely to get funded if your startup is simply a side project you're exploring while you maintain your full time job. Many founders view this as a "chicken or the egg" conundrum, as they feel that they can't go all-in and ditch their day job until they have some funding, but they can't get funding unless they're 100% focused on their startup. Remember, though, that you don't have to wait until you get funding to get started validating your business model. In fact, beginning to do so on the side while you still have a full time job is absolutely advisable, even as a side-project. Investors will be impressed that you've taken action versus simply putting pen to paper to write about a business. It's important, however, to make sure that your entire founding team is in complete alignment on what will be needed from them. Are they ready to step out and focus 100% of their efforts on the startup? Do they need to see the company receive a minimum amount of funding before they'll join full time? Or do they need to see a certain level of customer validation? Whatever it is, have this conversation with potential co-founders sooner rather than later.

The Big Takeaway

Rather than focus on perfecting your startup idea before you even have a team in place, realize that most investors consider the team to be the single most important aspect of a startup. Be thoughtful about what roles should exist on your initial startup team, and be honest with your partners and yourself about each person's expectations and commitment to the business.

An Investor's Perspective
Morris Wheeler, Drummond Road Capital

Morris Wheeler is a busy guy. The startup community in Cleveland, Ohio knows Morris as one of its most active and vocal members, one who serves as an angel investor and mentor to many area entrepreneurs. Yet, his presence is felt well beyond the Cleveland city limits, and even outside of Ohio. In fact, Morris lives in Colorado for several months of the year and is actively involved with Techstars Boulder and its surrounding startup community. His LinkedIn is agnostic when it comes to where he publicly pledges allegiance, citing his hometown as "wherever the good deals are." He means it, too — as CB Insights ranked his investment firm, Drummond Road Capital, as one of the most active seed investors of 2014.

When it comes to investing in technology-oriented startup teams, Morris is very specific about what he's looking for. In fact, he refers to the ultimate team as The Hacker, The Hipster, and The Suit – which is a variation of similar personas championed by investors Dave McClure and Micah Baldwin.

"The Hacker is the definitive technical lead inside of a startup, and this role is critical. I need to know that a technology-oriented startup company actually has technology within its roots. The Hipster is just as important, because it's not enough to simply be able to *develop* a product. Design and Product Management are vital, and The Hipster has a keen eye for these areas. The final member of the team is The Suit. This is somebody that understands the market, and can translate how the product can actually result in a viable, valuable business."

Morris doesn't suggest that an ideal startup team is necessarily made up of three *people*, but it must cover these three *functions*. It's possible that one person plays more than one role, but it's rare that one person can play all three. Morris believes so much in the concept of a startup *team*, that it's quite rare for him to even *consider* investing in a solo entrepreneur.

Of course, startup teams can't simply check the Hacker, Hipster, and Suit boxes off and plan on receiving a check from Drummond Road Capital. Proving that these three functions are accounted for just means that the team has passed the first hurdle. Aside from these functions, Morris believes that an ideal startup team must also possess the following characteristics:

Deep domain knowledge

If a team is creating software to help accountants be more productive, it better have somebody on it that has experience in accounting. Of course, there are ways to build up domain knowledge, even if you haven't spent ten years slogging it out in a specific industry. Bringing somebody on as an Advisor or co-founder is one way to instantly enjoy the benefits that comes along with having domain expertise.

Transparency with investors

It is usually a red flag for Morris if the CEO's background is deeply rooted in sales. Trust and transparency is important, especially in the beginning stages of a startup. There isn't room for any "spin."

Previous startup experience

This isn't to say that all (or any) of the startup team's members need to have started a company before. However, they must understand the level of commitment that it takes to actually leave a "day job" and jump into something as risky as a startup. At minimum, Morris looks for each team member to at least some experience working in a startup.

Real-world problem solving capabilities

Morris looks for "flexible intelligence" from startup teams – the ability to solve a problem, yet be nimble enough to listen to the market. He not only believes that it's possible for teams outside of Silicon Valley to be "flexibly intelligent," but he says that he may even see more teams outside of Silicon Valley who embody this characteristic. Of the teams that he's invested in that score well in this area, many actually come from the Midwest.

7. BUILD MILLION DOLLAR ALLIES

Aside from having the right founding team in place, it is just as critical to have a support system in place that can help see to it that you reach your goal of getting your new company funded.

It starts at home

The foundation of this necessary support system absolutely must start at home. If you're in a long-term committed relationship, your partner must be on board with your decision to take the leap and seek funding for your startup. The minute you take a dollar from an investor (let alone a million dollars), everything changes. Your commitment to your startup deepens, your professional responsibilities swell up, and personal time will begin to fade away. So before you go down any path that you think could lead to getting your startup funded and launched, be sure that you don't forget that your ally at home is the most important ally you will have.

Engaging Mentors and Advisors

You can build upon this foundation of support outside of the home with professional mentors. Mentors can come in many shapes and sizes. Engaging those who have gone through the process of starting a business and raising money from investors can be especially helpful. They are going to know the unique challenges that you're facing and can draw on their experience to help you avoid potential pitfalls. They can also add credibility to your startup when speaking on your behalf to others – whether to investors, potential partners, and even customers.

If you already have strong relationships with mentors who have "been there and done that", engage them immediately. Share your vision for your startup and consider gauging their interest in becoming even more deeply involved as an Advisor. An Advisor can be a mentor, but should be willing to take on a more active role in helping you push your business forward. Even if your relationship with this person is strong, it's important to be specific with them about needs and expectations, as well as what you may be able to offer in return. Many Advisors may be perfectly okay with meeting weekly and may expect nothing in return. In fact, in my experience, I've learned that most mentors get involved to be helpful and aren't incentivized by anything other than seeing you succeed.

Some Advisors prefer to formalize their involvement in exchange for equity or stock options. There's nothing necessarily wrong with this, but it will be up to you to gauge what you need and whether the value the mentor brings is in line with what you're giving up. Formal Advisors generally receive anything between 0.25% - 1% (if anything at all) in equity, which may vest over the course of 1-2 years. Some Advisors might require a bit more. If you do decide to give more, don't be afraid to hold your Advisors to milestone-based commitments. If their role as an Advisor is to open up doors for you, then getting them to agree to initiate a certain number of conversations each quarter isn't out of the question. While it might be difficult to part with any equity to a non-investor, remember that 1% of zero is zero. Sharing a modest amount of equity with Advisors who can be instrumental in helping you get your business funded is a no-brainer if you believe you wouldn't have been able to do so otherwise.

If you don't have a strong network of mentors to turn to, you're actually not alone. Not everybody enjoys solid relationships with people they consider to be professional mentors. Mentor relationships can take years to cultivate. Similar to the other personal relationships you have in your life with close friends, relationships with mentors are based on trust and a strong intellectual and emotional connection. It's not as simple as approaching a professional and simply asking them to be your mentor. The good news is that if you're starting from scratch in developing your own mentor network, there are steps that you can start to take right now to find the right mentors and begin to engage with them:

Rekindle past relationships

Do you have a former employer or colleague whom you respect and trust? While it would be ideal if they've gone through the process of raising startup funding, you can still learn from those who haven't. Share your goals and aspirations with them. Aside from receiving guidance, you might find that they know people who can help you and can facilitate introductions on your behalf.

Reach out to leaders within in your startup community with whom you identify with the most.

Whose startup path do you find yourself modeling yours after? Which startup community members are you most drawn to? Remember, it's okay to ask these individuals if you can buy them a cup of coffee. Consider it a "mentor date." Just like a real date, you can use the time to share more about yourself, learn about them, and determine whether a real connection exists. If it does, you may have found a mentor with whom you can begin to engage with regularly.

Learn about formal programs that may exist.

Accelerators, incubators, and other programs often will match startups with mentors within their network. Research the service organizations within your startup community to understand whether programs like this exist. Keep in mind that even in a "mentor matching" program, real mentors are people with whom you have a strong connection and relationship. Just because you've been formally assigned a mentor doesn't make that person a true mentor. However, meeting potential mentors through formalized programs is often a more efficient way to screen Advisors and, often times, one or two of the connections may result in true mentor relationships.

The Big Takeaway

When launching eFuneral, the mentors who were most helpful to us were those that we had personally known for years. They were helpful in many ways – from helping us hash out the business model to making connections to other investors and even attending a couple of early customer development meetings. Having them involved added credibility to our venture and allowed others to take us more seriously.

Finding strong mentors should be about more than helping get your startup funded. These are real relationships that can lead to potential introductions, can help you solve problems you run into, and can generally serve as a sounding board to you. More than that, these relationships can stay with you for life.

An Entrepreneur's Perspective
John Knific, Decision Desk

When John Knific was boarding his flight to Zurich to perform a paid gig as a jazz pianist (while still in college!), he did not realize that his life would be filled with board meetings and investor pitches just a few years later. As a college student, John took his passion for music – combined with the frustrations he experienced auditioning for performing arts programs – to create Decision Desk, a platform that facilitates communication between academic institutions and applicants during the application process. Before he knew it, his piano was swapped out for a MacBook and he was on his way to building a real business. Today, Decision Desk is used by hundreds of higher education organizations such as the University of Michigan, Oberlin College, and the Rhodes Trust, as well as others, to receive and review student applications.

John credits much of the success he's had with Decision Desk to his ability to establish strong relationships with mentors early on in his career. He considers his own startup community of Cleveland, Ohio to be a factor in his ability to establish those relationships.

"People want to see startups succeed here in Cleveland. Early on in my career, I was able to find local mentors who really wanted to see me succeed as a young founder. Most of my mentors are entrepreneurs themselves and, by helping me, they saw an opportunity to pay it forward and help somebody the same way that they were helped in the past. In Cleveland, people really look out for each other in this respect."

If one wants to build a mentor relationship, how would you go about doing that? John says that in a place like Cleveland, all you have to do is ask.

"The city is small enough where if you really wanted to sit down with somebody for coffee, chances are that you have some common connection who would be willing to introduce the two of you. But even if you don't have a common connection, Cleveland is the kind of place where it's not uncommon for an out-of-the-blue phone call or email from a young founder to result in a coffee meeting with a more experienced member of the startup community. You just have to be bold enough to ask. Now, when other founders reach out to me, my natural reaction is to meet with them and get to know them."

8. ENVISION YOUR DREAM TEAM OF INVESTORS

If you're trying to raise $1 Million for your startup and you're starting from scratch, it might feel like anybody that's willing to write a check is your "target market" of investors. While you might be willing to take an investment from anybody that's willing to invest (although as we'll soon discuss, this could be a mistake) – that doesn't necessarily mean that your target market of investors includes everybody. Just like there's a specific audience for the unique product or service you're trying to launch, it's also true that there's a unique, target investor base for your company.

Before you begin pitching just anybody, sit down and outline the ideal investor types you want on your team. Different types of investors add value in different ways, aside from the amount of hard cash invested. Consider the following investor types and think about which are right for your business:

Market-oriented investors

These investors generally like to invest in markets that they know and are familiar with. This type of investor may have had deep operating experience within your market or simply have made numerous investments in similar types of businesses. Finding and securing market-oriented investors is a double-edged sword, because while you may be able to catch an investor's interest because of their familiarity with the market you're operating in or the type of business that you're building, you will not be able to pull a fast one on them. You'd better know and understand your business and market well.

Market-oriented investors can be extremely beneficial, since aside from money, they offer experience and may even be able to make helpful connections with customers or potential partners. If their reputation within the market is strong, they can also boost your credibility and relevance.

Function-oriented investors

Despite building out your "million dollar team," it's highly unlikely that you have expertise in every functional area. Make an honest assessment of what skills your team lacks. Is search engine marketing critical to your company's success? Do you foresee your company needing to become a thought leader through content marketing? Consider targeting investors who are experts at the functional areas missing on your team.

Function-oriented investors can help you dig in and educate your team members in the area of their expertise. They may not be a specialist in your market per se, but you can apply what you learn from them and combine that with the market-insights you're already learning on your own and from the market experts that are on your Advisory board.

Funding-oriented investors

Even when you close your initial $1 Million funding round, you'll quickly realize that you may need to continue raising additional rounds of funding, especially if you plan to quickly scale your business. While the investors you initially raise money from may want to participate in future rounds of funding, you'll also likely need to find larger sources of capital who can lead these follow-on rounds. While your $1 Million round of funding may be comprised of mostly individuals, future rounds of funding may start to involve venture capital funds or other types of institutional investors.

Which investors are closely tied to larger venture capital groups that may be willing to lead a future funding round for you? Do you know who has co-invested with that particular investor? How familiar are they with the fundraising process after the initial seed round? Make it a point to include investors who have a strong familiarity with post-seed fundraising in your initial group.

Another way that a funding-oriented investor can help is to actually drive up the valuation of your startup. Particularly if that investor has a strong network and is viewed by other investors as an influencer, it's possible for one single investor to open up quite a few doors. When other investors see that an influential investor has given you money, your startup may become a more attractive investment. Jason Calacanis, a startup founder and angel investor in Silicon Valley, suggests that Gary Vaynerchuk and Chris Sacca are examples of influential investors. However, realize that every market has their own influential investors that may not necessarily be household names to all, but are well known to the investors in that market.

It should be noted that the investor types above aren't necessarily mutually exclusive. There can certainly be an investor who has duel expertise. For instance, an investor can know a specific market and also be an expert at venture law – *and* even has strong ties to follow-on funders. Yet, you'll likely find that the primary value that an investor adds fits pretty neatly into one of the above categories.

But, how do you know if an investor *truly* adds value?

Nearly all investors like to consider themselves "value added" investors. Unfortunately, their definition of "value added" may not line up with yours. Some investors like to think of themselves as being "involved," where others might consider it to be meddling. The best sources of information to find out whether an investor actually does add value beyond the capital that they contribute is to talk to the startups that they've actually invested in. Other founders can easily tell you which of their investors have been the most helpful and can explain what it's like to work with that investor.

Don't just put anybody on the list

When you're building out your "Dream Team" of investors, remember that you should be putting together your *ideal* list of investor types, not just anybody you think will invest. This is why, more often than not, friends and family likely won't be this list – not unless they actually add real value and fit into one of the investor types above.

This doesn't mean you absolutely shouldn't take investment from friends and family. It may even be necessary in the very beginning. But consciously think of investors who proactively add value. The stereotypical "rich uncle" may be willing to give you money, but if he doesn't have relevant expertise, isn't familiar with your market, has no connections to downstream investment, and doesn't add any value aside from the dollars he's contributing, then he really doesn't belong.

Should you avoid investment from friends and family altogether? That's certainly a personal question that you'll need to answer yourself. Sometimes, friends and family can be the most supportive bunch and it can be a signal to more professional investors that you're unafraid to do whatever it takes to see your startup succeed. In other cases, it can make Thanksgiving dinner very awkward, especially if their expectations aren't aligned with yours. Consider these relationships and ultimately only consider accepting money from friends and family once you know they will not be dramatically impacted should they lose every single cent of their investment. Be up front about the fact that this investment will likely be the riskiest one they'll ever make, and that they should assume they won't ever see their investment pay off. If they're still up for taking the risk and you trust in the relationship, they may be the type of friend or family member from whom you can consider accepting an investment.

The Big Takeaway

You've likely spent a great deal of time and put a lot of thought into figuring out who your ideal customers will be. Given that your initial investors will have a significant role in helping you launch and shape your business, be thoughtful about who you invite into this circle. While you may feel obligated to take investment money from anyone who's willing to write a check, understand that not all investors are necessarily created equal in the value they bring to your startup.

An Investor's Perspective
Ian Sigalow, Greycroft Partners

If you're hustling down Madison Avenue trying to keep up with Ian Sigalow as he sprints from one meeting to another and back to the offices of Greycroft, the venture capital firm he co-founded, you'll likely notice that he shares a lot in common with other members of the New York startup community. He's pressed for time and always on the go. However, he is still very willing (and even eager!) to meet up-and-coming company founders. How else is he going to find that next big venture to invest in? Ian's firm is regarded as one of the top venture investors, not just in New York, but also in the United States and abroad. Yet, while many people view Ian as a New York investor, Ian's roots are based in the Midwest; he grew up in Akron, Ohio.

Whether a startup is based in Akron or New York, Ian believes it's important to think outside of one's immediate geography because we live in a world where the borders have blurred.

"Most startups don't have the luxury to only think about their own local startup community when trying to find funding. It's a good place to start, but most venture investors are looking for big opportunities regardless of where the startup is actually operating." While it may be daunting to network in a startup community that isn't your own, Ian believes that not having a strong network is simply a poor excuse in a day and age where everybody is connected to one another within just a few mutual connections.

"It's true that the majority of investments our firm makes start with a warm introduction from somebody we know. However, many times founders we meet with have to really work for an introduction. They take initiative – learning, for example, that a friend of theirs has a brother who has a company that we invested in and they find a way to get that person to introduce us. I'm certain that nobody is separated from me by more than a few degrees. It's not as hard as you would think to find a way to get introduced to me. For those that don't have those connections, they have to make them. I'm interested in meeting founders who are resourceful."

With that as a backdrop, if one isn't limited to his or her own startup community to find investors for their startup company, how is an entrepreneur to know which investors they should start reaching out to? Having the whole universe open to you seems daunting. How does an entrepreneur know how to really target those investors who are right for their startup?

"The personal connection between a founder and the individual partner at the investment firm who's leading the investment in them is critical. For founders who are fortunate enough to find multiple investors who can invest in their company, they have to trust their gut. Money aside, who do they really want to work with over the course of the next several years? Founders shouldn't forget that there will be a working relationship between them and the partner. What entrepreneurs should really look for is a partner who is just as passionate about the potential for their business as they are. That in itself is going to help the entrepreneur much more than the brand name of the investment firm that's writing the check."

9. READY, AIM...

A big part of landing the funding you need for your startup is making sure you're ready to have conversations with people who can actually write checks. Everything you've done thus far has been in preparation for the opportunity to pitch to investors. Do they expect you to walk them through a 20-slide Pitch Deck? Or is it 10 slides? How can you know the best way to tell your story in the most efficient, yet exciting, way possible?

Much like planning for Sunday's football game, in advance of proactively reaching out to investors you'll want to put together your playbook. The materials and documents that make up your playbook will vary depending on the type of business you have, but consider having some of the following in place before actively reaching out to investors:

Single-Page Startup Canvas

Likelihood someone will ask to see this: Low

Importance to complete before fundraising: Medium to High

A single page startup canvas is a great tool to help you get your business model documented simply on a single piece of paper. There are several different approaches to a canvas, from the original Business Model Canvas developed by Alexander Osterwalder to the Lean Canvas variation developed by Ash Maurya. There is a lot of great information online about how to best use a single-page startup canvas. Angel investors and VC's may not ask for this, but they're likely to be familiar with the concept (and many accelerators encourage startups to create one as an early exercise). Additionally, completing a single-page startup canvas is a simple enough exercise that forces you to ask yourself important questions about your startup and business model.

Summary: This is more of an exercise for you than for your investors, but it is simple enough to do. Completing it before beginning serious fundraising discussions with investors is a no-brainer.

Executive Summary

Likelihood someone will ask to see this: High

Importance to complete before fundraising: High

An executive summary is a boiled-down business plan. It covers the essentials: Problem/Solution, Market Size/Opportunity, Business/Revenue model, Team Bios, Financial Overview. However, instead of multiple pages for each section, this is expected to be much more succinct. The entire executive summary should be no more than a few pages at maximum. In fact, some institutional investors set a 2-page cap on executive summaries before agreeing to read them. It's pretty common for angel investors and VC's to ask for this, so have this ready before engaging them.

Summary: The sad reality is that they'll likely get glossed over, at best. But again, it sometimes is the admission ticket to even having an initial conversation.

Financial Model

Likelihood someone will ask to see this: Medium to High

Importance to complete before fundraising: High

This is one document that is much more necessary when fundraising outside of Silicon Valley, especially in more traditional "conservative" markets. Investors are investing in *businesses* and they care very much about how your startup can evolve into an actual business. It's not enough to "figure that part out later once traffic is high." As discussed in Chapter Two, you don't need to be a PhD in statistics to give investors what they need. Keep things simple, and show how a dollar invested (and spent) in your business can result in several dollars of revenue. You should also show why the total amount of capital that you're raising is necessary and what that money will get you. Investors want to know that there is a *purpose* behind the investment that they're making. Even for your own sake, you should understand what you really need, and how the capital will help you.

A word of caution: If you send a financial model ahead of a meeting, investors *will* ask about it. If your financial model changes (and it will), investors *will* want to know why. If you base your financial model on a few major assumptions, call those assumptions out and highlight them for the investor. This way, when figures change, it will make the conversation more manageable.

Summary: Not only is this necessary for investors, but you better have a strong handle on your business before expecting to raise a million dollars in seed funding. It's no excuse if you're not a "business guy" or "numbers woman" by trade – if it's your startup, then there's no excuse for you to not be well versed on the financials.

Pitch Deck

Likelihood someone will ask to see this: High

Importance to complete before fundraising: High

The Pitch Deck has essentially replaced the business plan as the single most common item that investors typically ask for in order to consider investing. A Pitch Deck is usually a Powerpoint or Keynote presentation that covers similar areas outlined in the Executive Summary, but in a more visual form with 1-2 slides highlighting each critical component of the business. Many people prefer to maintain two different Pitch Decks: one that is sent ahead of time that can stand on its own without additional context, and another that is more visual, but is intended to be presented in person. Keep in mind that while Pitch Decks are meant to present the business opportunity in a compelling way, it's not necessary to be a graphic designer to create a Pitch Deck that investors will appreciate. Following Guy Kawasaki's advice of the 10/20/30 rule – 10 slides (max), presented in 20 minutes, using a 30-point (or bigger) font – will help you craft a proper Pitch

Deck. For the version of the Pitch Deck that you present in person, don't forget to include addendum slides. These slides are akin to a website's FAQ's. They're not front-and-center and may never get used during a presentation unless a certain question is asked. If you've prepared appropriately, you can simply jump ahead to the relevant addendum slide and address the question head-on. Finally, be focused and concise. This deck is meant to present the overview of the market and your business's potential in just a few slides. Don't waste any time (or space) with ramblings that aren't relevant to investors.

Summary: The Pitch Deck is a must these days, both inside and outside of Silicon Valley. Don't worry about paying a graphic designer, though. You can create a simple, yet compelling Pitch Deck using Google Images incorporated into a basic Powerpoint or Keynote template. Slideshare is a great resource for sample Pitch Decks, which might give you some inspiration or at least a bit of guidance on format.

Prototype

Likelihood someone will ask to see this: Medium

Importance to complete before fundraising: Medium to High

There's a term for a software product that is announced, yet never ends up seeing the light of day in the marketplace: vaporware. The fear that many investors have when considering to invest in a technology based business is that their investment will simply fall into a hole and the "next best idea" that was pitched to them never develops into anything. A prototype, whether for a physical product or a tech-based product, is one way that you can calm some of these fears, even if the product is not much more than vaporware. Some investors will insist on seeing a prototype, because while everybody can have a great idea and convince a savvy marketer friend to help them cobble together a seemingly sound plan for the business, it's difficult to tell whether the actual product can be produced. Even then, it can be hard to envision just how compelling the product can be until it's experienced, even if it's just a demonstration. For some investors, seeing is believing and the prototype trumps the Pitch Deck, executive summary, and anything else you would put in front of them.

Summary: Not all investors will require a prototype, but you certainly have a much better chance of catching their attention if you have a compelling one built out.

Functional Beta Product

Likelihood someone will ask to see this: Medium

Importance to complete before fundraising: Low to Medium

Many people have different definitions of what a Beta product actually is. For the purposes of this discussion, let's define a Beta product as something that is just basic enough to be a functional product. It serves its purpose but all parties (including the customers) know that it is just the first iteration and will likely evolve quite a bit. The importance of this category is set to low-to-medium, not because it's not important to build a functional product. Indeed if you can build one, you should consider doing so. But in the context of raising money for your startup it's not altogether necessary. In fact, it sometimes can have an adverse effect. On one hand, investors want to see that you have traction. Certainly, a product that exists in the marketplace and that is being used by real customers is one way to prove this. However, the allure of "pre-launch" status to investors is real even outside of Silicon Valley. If a product has launched – even in Beta – and isn't immediately a hit, it could raise questions from certain investors. This isn't necessarily fair to the startup founder, as quick hits are relatively rare. Yet, it's still a reality. If your intent is to raise funding for your startup, keep this in mind. As you target investors, get a sense of whether the majority of their investments were made to companies prior to their product launch, or after. This will help you know whether having a functional beta will impact your ability to raise funds.

Summary: I would never recommend that founders shouldn't make building and releasing their first iteration of their product a priority. Still, it's important to know that certain investors are attracted to "pre-launch" stage companies. Target these investors early, even before you've released your product.

Business Plan

Likelihood someone will ask to see this: Medium

Importance to complete before fundraising: Low to Medium

The days of submitting 50-page business plans in order to be considered for seed stage investment are almost over. In Silicon Valley, they're completely over. However, outside of Silicon Valley, it could still be possible to receive a request for something like this, particularly from governmental organizations that offer loans or grants to startups. Regardless, spending all sorts of time on a bulky business plan is not the right priority for the very beginning of a startup and certainly shouldn't take priority over a Pitch Deck, prototype, or executive summary. However, this isn't to say that a Business Plan is altogether pointless. While it might not be necessary for raising your first million dollars of investment, it still is a useful exercise for a startup founder to go through after spending time validating the pieces of the overall plan.

Summary: This is mostly an obsolete document when raising initial investment dollars. However, keep in mind that more conservative groups, like government entities and nonprofits, may still require a variation of a Business Plan.

The Big Takeaway

While you might engage with people who could ultimately become investors in your business, you should have certain things in order before you really start engaging potential investors. Know that investors may ask for any of the items outlined in this section, so be prepared to either provide them with what they're looking for, or have a good reason as to why you can't.

An Investor's Perspective
Tige Savage, Revolution Ventures

Many of today's angel and venture capital investors are relatively new to the profession of investing in technology startups. The majority can't intimately recall the dot-com bust in 1999, because they weren't yet making investments. That's not the case with Tige Savage. Since

1998, Tige has served as a venture executive with Riggs Capital Partners, Time Warner Ventures, and more recently, Revolution Ventures where he leads the venture group alongside former AOL CEO and Chairman, Steve Case. He's led investments in groups like FlexCar/ZipCar, LivingSocial, Revolution Money and dozens of others. To call Tige an industry veteran would be an understatement.

If you're pursuing startup capital from Revolution Ventures, you don't have to be located in Silicon Valley. In fact, Tige notes that the Washington D.C., based firm deploys 80% of its capital to startups *outside* of Silicon Valley.

"We think that Silicon Valley is a terrific place to start a technology company. It's just not the only place. There were certainly early technology startup successes in the Bay Area, and as a result, more resources and capital have become available to entrepreneurs. But there are other geographies that are uniquely situated to provide advantages to entrepreneurs. For instance, if you want to start an automotive technology based business you might want to consider Detroit. If you're launching a cyber-security data startup, locating to Washington D.C. to have the NSA nearby could be a great move. The reality is that great entrepreneurs can start great companies anywhere. We like to see entrepreneurs locate themselves where the cards are stacked most for success, wherever that may be."

In order to access the $200 Million in capital that Revolution has available in its current fund, entrepreneurs better be sure they're prepared. And the first part of being prepared is being able to answer a couple of simple questions.

"When we're considering investing in a startup, we first want to know that the entrepreneur has a clear understanding of the market. Who are the major players? What about this market is ripe for disruption? What is this startup's unfair advantage to disrupt this market? In the first conversation we have with a company, these are questions that we're looking for clear answers to."

Of course, an entrepreneur who only boasts advantages and doesn't recognize real weaknesses could be showing their ignorance.

"No team is perfect. We do want to know what the startup *doesn't* have yet, and what the startup is planning to do to address that need. Often times, it's something that we might be able to help with. After all, the value we add goes beyond the capital we're contributing. We want to work with entrepreneurs who are just as honest about their weaknesses as they are with their strengths so we know how we can truly help them."

When pitching to Revolution Ventures, it's a good idea to have your Pitch Deck and Executive Summary in place. But more important than the actual documents is the story behind the documents.

"At the seed stage, it's important that the entrepreneur create a reasonably clear path for inflection. What are the important milestones your startup needs to achieve with the initial seed capital in order to understand that you have a business that will scale? What needs to happen in order to achieve these milestones? What will the business need to look like in order to do those things? Whether it's the executive summary or Pitch Deck – these questions should be answered and articulated to make it easy for investors to understand how the business can and will grow."

Being prepared doesn't just include understanding your market and charting the potential growth of your business. Investing is a two-way street. Entrepreneurs should be careful to also research their investors.

"It's pretty well documented that we like to make investments in certain types of businesses. If an entrepreneur is approaching us about investing in their business and it's so different from the types of startups we typically invest in – it just shows that they haven't really done their homework on us. Not knowing who we are and the type of venture investments we make causes us to question the entrepreneur's ability to pay attention to the details, which is an obvious red-flag."

Revolution Ventures is just another prime example of capital – and lots of it – being available to technology startup entrepreneurs no matter where they're located... so long as they're adequately prepared.

10. MAKE YOUR OWN CONNECTIONS

Some people quickly dismiss the idea of raising capital for their startup because of a saying that they've heard time and time again: "It's all about who you know." They make excuses such as,

"I'm not that well connected, I don't even know any investors."

"I don't have rich friends and family."

"This isn't Silicon Valley. There aren't investors everywhere you turn."

While it's true that raising capital for your startup will require investors and those investors simply aren't going to reach out to you and hand over a check unsolicited, it's *not* the case that you have to be super well connected or move your company to the Bay Area to find investors for your startup.

At eFuneral, over 2/3 of the total funds we raised came from sources who we did not know prior to starting eFuneral. We did leverage our personal networks to raise 1/3 of what we raised, but the bulk of the funds came from connections we made on our own through networking and, essentially, cold-calling.

In order for you to cultivate a supportive group of investors, there are a few things you can do right now:

Keep your allies (and other people you know) engaged.

For those of you who already have great mentors in your life, this is usually the best place to start. As we discussed in Chapter Five, having a stable of helpful allies is critical as you go through this process. Once you begin to engage with this group, you should see their level of excitement over your concept grow. If you don't, you may want to pause and understand why. After all, these are the people that have a personal interest in you and should genuinely want to help. If they don't seem that excited about your business, probe to find out why. They could have critical feedback that you need to hear.

Let's assume that their enthusiasm levels are very high. What should you do next?

First, keep in mind that these allies could make for ideal first investors. We'll discuss later on how you may be able to go about asking for that first dollar of investment from this particular group.

As I mentioned earlier, these allies can be critical in introducing you to the right people within your own startup community. However, it's important to know how to ask for an introduction. It's likely your allies are successful businesspeople in their own right, which usually means that they're constantly on the go, with busy schedules, and much on their minds. Know that you're competing with other people and tasks for their "mind share." Because your company is most likely not on their mind 100% of the time, you'll need to help them help you.

Rather than asking them, "Do you know any investors I should talk to?" – do the legwork yourself and ask them to connect you to *specific* individuals. There are a couple of great resources that you can use to help you when you're doing this legwork:

AngelList

AngelList is an online portal that allows startups to engage virtually with potential investors. AngelList has become a popular place for investors to list their current and prior investments, and to share information about themselves. Currently, this tool seems to be more popular inside of Silicon Valley, however, investors outside of Silicon Valley are beginning to use the platform in increasing numbers. I suggest that you make a list of those investors that hold a place on your "Dream Team." While it's pretty easy to reach out directly through the AngelList platform, don't – at least not quite yet.

Crunchbase

Crunchbase is a free website that profiles startups as well as their investors. When using Crunchbase, search specifically for the startups that are located in your area (no matter what type of business) – as well as startups that operate in the same general industry as your startup. Local startups often raise money from local investors, and those investors are often looking for the next hot local startup to invest in.

Don't limit yourself to raising capital only from local investors. Investors who are interested in your specific type of business are located everywhere, and you should figure out how to connect with them using the tools you have at your disposal. Investors very familiar with your industry can be tricky, though. On one hand, you know that they're interested in the type of business you're building. On the other hand, information that you share with them could get back to another company they've invested in within that category, so you need to be careful with the type of information you disclose.

Local Angel Investor Networks

Research local angel investor networks to find out who their members are. Angel investor networks work in a couple of different ways. Some have committed funds that make investments on behalf of their members, while others act as a source of deal flow and due diligence for a group of active angel investors who ultimately make their own investment decisions. While you can engage with the angel investor group as a whole (and we'll discuss this later), try to find the member list of the particular angel investor group in your area so you can research these individuals' specific backgrounds.

LinkedIn

LinkedIn is a great tool you can use to determine if your allies – or anybody else in your network – are connected to your "Dream Team" investor group. The first (and simplest) thing you can do is search for specific individual investors. You can do this with investor names you've compiled from sources like AngelList, Crunchbase, and angel investor group member lists -- along with anybody else that you want on your "Dream Team." Once you've found a particular LinkedIn profile page, you can check to see if you have any second level connections. If you do, then you can engage with your mentor, ally, or whoever else that's connected with this individual and ask them for a personal introduction. Another way you can use LinkedIn is to simply search for the term "Investor" as a keyword within the Advanced Search settings. You can customize this your search further by location (using the keyword "Investor" and inputting your local zip code) or by adding other keywords that are relevant to your startup (to find market or function oriented investors).

Have you identified potential investors, but can't find any mutual connections that could provide an introduction?

Behold the cold call (and make it a bit warmer).

Cold calling is known to send shivers up the spines of those who don't consider themselves to be skilled at networking. In sales, especially, cold calling is brutal but necessary. When trying to attract investment for your startup – cold calling is also often a necessary process. But it's not something that you should be scared of. And quite often, it doesn't even involve an actual *call*.

Social media can make a cold call a little bit warmer. Raising funds for your startup is a process, and it isn't going to happen all at once. Now that you've identified your target investor list, you can start by engaging with them on social media channels like Twitter. Participate in conversations that they're having. Answer questions that they post. Comment on posts that they make within their blog (if they have one). Your first communication with them shouldn't be to ask for investment. Let them get to know you a bit – even if it is in a small way. Then, when you're ready to have an introductory conversation with them, you can send a well-crafted email. If they're at least somewhat familiar with you, you're much more likely to receive a response back.

In our particular case, David Cohen, who you heard from earlier in the book, performed fairly extensive due diligence on eFuneral.

Many entrepreneurs and technology investors are quite familiar with David and his successful investments. However, we had no direct connection to David. Despite that, we had a series of emails and phone calls with him, getting feedback about our business as he was doing his due diligence. Ultimately, he chose not to invest. But the time we spent with him turned into the start of a relationship (and is one of the reasons why David agreed to be featured in this book!)

How did it all start? One single tweet.

Of course, it wasn't *really* just one tweet. I had engaged with him via Twitter several times, often receiving responses back immediately. After several weeks, I finally asked if he would be interested in reviewing our demo. He then invited me to email him directly, and set up time to talk via his assistant.

If I had not taken the time to engage with David on social media for several weeks, would he have accepted my cold-email and reviewed my demo? Possibly – but the odds were a lot lower. Yet, because David had some familiarity with me, it increased my chances and led to the conversations we ultimately had.

Shake some hands

Utilize the allies in your own startup community. As you've already begun to build connections in your startup community (as discussed in Chapter Three), leverage them. Consider other startup founders who are fundraising to be allies as well. You might be surprised by which connections will actually lead to other helpful connections. After all, when it comes to finding investors for your startup, it's always best to leave no stone unturned. The connection to your next investor might come from an unexpected, unlikely place.

The Big Takeaway

The reality is that it *does* take connections in order to secure investment for your startup. But this doesn't mean that you have to already be connected to well known, deep-pocketed investors. You may already be more connected to potential investors than you'd expect. The Internet can provide a wealth of information about specific investors and even facilitate introductions. If the connections aren't there, platforms like LinkedIn and Twitter allow you to build your *own* connections in a non-obtrusive way.

An Entrepreneur's Perspective
Ed Buchholz, ExpenseBot

Ed Buchholz's family is probably not at all surprised to see that he has developed into an entrepreneur. Even at a young age, Ed was exposed to the ups and downs that come along with owning a business; he had a front row seat watching his father operate the family plumbing business, a company that's been in the family for generations. As Ed got older, he found himself being more attracted to work involving computers rather than wrenches and cable augers. While in college at Bowling Green State University, Ed earned extra money by working in the computer lab, and later, in the school's network operations center. While still in school, when he came across an ad for a Customer Service role working at a small technology company, not even Ed realized that the job he was applying for (and would later be offered) would lead him to the world of high-growth technology startups. But after progressive technology oriented roles at that company and well-timed promotions – that's exactly the path Ed found himself on. He went on to be a part of several startups and even founded two of his own.

Today, Ed is the Co-Founder and CEO of ExpenseBot, a technology startup that uses machine learning to allow "expense reports to do themselves." Ed grew up in Ohio and, yes, investors in Ohio have funded Ed's businesses. But Ed was able to navigate investor networks in places like Chicago, San Francisco, Silicon Valley, and Boulder, Colorado as well.

"We were able to raise money from people that we personally knew in Ohio, but we also knew that we couldn't confine ourselves to Ohio. We actively traveled from coast to coast in order to network. Of course, given that we didn't have strong networks in many of those places already, it was a challenge. So we did things to stand out. In fact, one of the first meetings we had with a Venture Capital group was the result of a tweet I sent out directly to one of the partners at the Chicago-based firm. We got an invitation to come to their offices the next day."

The Venture Capital group that Ed tweeted to? Lightbank, a firm whose founders helped start Groupon. That meeting resulted in Ed's company receiving a major investment offer almost on the spot. It came at a good time, too. Just 24 hours earlier, Ed's company's bank account balance had reached a dangerously low point.

"That meeting wouldn't have happened if we just rested on our laurels and relied solely on the relationships we already had. We had to work to build new relationships, even from a distance. Today, my current company, ExpenseBot, has investors from Ohio, Colorado, and even Israel. Even though we now have a solid network, we're constantly trying to build upon it."

Today, ExpenseBot is a fast-growing startup in Cleveland, Ohio after having participated in the Techstars Boulder class of 2014.

11. CROSSING THE ONE DOLLAR BARRIER

When you are fundraising for your startup, the hardest dollar to raise is often the first. This is also true for sales once you launch your business – something to keep in mind down the road! There are a few reasons why the first dollar can be the most difficult:

It's scary to ask for it.

It's not necessarily hard to ask for it, it's just scary. Many first-time founders of tech startups are most often technically skilled themselves. Business skills, however, are often lacking. In these cases, it's not uncommon that the founder has *never* had to ask anybody they didn't know to hand over a large amount of cash. Even founders with backgrounds in sales and business development understand that soliciting capital from investors is a much different proposition than selling a product to a customer. It's understandable that startup fundraising can be a scary proposition, but founders must resolve to overcome this fear in order to attain the funding they need.

Not many investors like to be first.

I often joke that investors are very similar to sheep. They don't like to lead, they like to follow…and then move in herds. Rarely, you'll find investors who are so confident in themselves and the investments that they make, that they take pride in investing the first dollar into a startup. For the investors who do it, it's part bravado, and part strategy. If the company is successful, this first dollar in often earns them the right to continue to invest in future fundraise rounds.

Many investors are interested in the "social proof" that you have, influenced by the fact that other investors have already invested in your company. They'll ask you which other investors have already committed. If there are none, they could take that as a sign that your company isn't worthy of investment. If you already have several investors, others will likely view that as a vote of confidence in you; it partially "de-risks" the opportunity.

Despite the fears that many founders have in asking for that first dollar, getting that dollar of investment is so important. It can create a domino effect that leads to other people investing.

So, how do you get that first dollar?

The first check you receive should have your signature on it.

If you're asking investors to hand you $1 million, you had better be prepared to consider yourself the first investor. In Chapter Four, we discussed the importance of being "all in" on your startup. Again, this doesn't mean putting a second mortgage on your home, or selling your car and relying solely on public transportation (although, there are plenty of entrepreneurs who have done just that in order to see their startup dreams realized). You should be able to show that you're making a serious investment in the business relative to your means. Even if you can only afford to contribute just $500, making a meaningful contribution is a sign to investors that you're serious about your startup. Perhaps you're not literally writing a check, but you're investing by giving up your well paying job and willing to take a below-market salary until the business is more proven. Regardless, you should be able to show that you're making a serious investment into your own business.

Move on to your family, friends, and mentors.

The best shot at receiving an initial investment check will come from the people who personally know you. Often times, this leads people to think about their friends and family. This *could* be an option for you, but as we discussed in Chapter Six – this can also be tricky. If you have friends and family who have made these types of investments in the past, or who fall into one of the investor types that make up your "Dream Team," certainly they could make for attractive early investors. If this is the case, be sure that they are aware of what they're actually signing up for and understand the high risk nature of their investment.

Beyond family and friends, though, think closely about your mentors. Did you find one or two who are particularly excited about your startup? They could make great candidates to approach for investment, particularly if they've had previous startup experience. Consider asking one of your mentors to be your *first* investor, even if the check they're writing is relatively small. If they say no, ask them to be candid with you as to why. Chances are this conversation will be one of the most beneficial and eye opening on your journey. In it, you may learn:

Are they not as excited about your startup's prospects as you thought they were – or that they led you to believe?

Are they simply not making any more startup investments?

Are they not the type who likes to be "first investor in" – but prefers the extra security of knowing that other investors have committed to invest alongside them?

If you find out that they're not as excited as you thought about your business, this could be another good moment to pause to reflect a bit and take in the feedback that they have to offer.

If they're not making any more startup investments due to a change in investment strategy or a major life event, it's also good for you to know so you can explain it to others; after all a "cheerleader" with money should ultimately become an investor. If they don't, others may take this as a bad sign. This will take finesse. You might consider asking "cheerleaders-who-won't-invest" if they'd be willing to speak directly to potential investors who know them to tell their story in their own words.

All hope is not lost if they don't like to be the first investment in a startup. In fact, they've presented you with a major opportunity.

Ask investors to follow each other.

When you learn of an investor who prefers to invest alongside others, you can suggest that they consider investing *contingent* on you securing a matching investment from another investor. This means that you can receive a commitment from them, but not take their actual check unless you're able to find another investor who is willing to come on board as an investor under the same terms. For the investor who is genuinely interested but doesn't like to lead, this can be a winning proposition. They can get early access, but their risk can be tempered a bit knowing that somebody else will be making the same commitment. As you talk to other allies and potential investors, lead with the fact that you have an investor ready to write a check if they're willing to match. What's great about this approach is that when you finally find that match, you don't *just* have your first investor; you have your *first two* investors.

At eFuneral, we leveraged the investor-match approach in the very beginning to build investment momentum, which created a bit of a domino effect in our initial fundraising effort. We were fortunate enough to have two close mentors (Christopher and Tim) to guide us early on. We leveraged the potential of joining the 10xelerator when we asked them to invest, with the investment being contingent on two things:

First, we would quit our full-time jobs and dedicate ourselves to eFuneral. Next, we had to get accepted into the 10xelerator and receive the $20,000 grant.

Both agreed – and once we were accepted into the accelerator, we not only had the $20,000 earned from the accelerator grant – but we now had *$60,000* in total funding. It wasn't all we intended to raise, but it gave us a great start.

The Big Takeaway

Asking for money can be scary and awkward, but it's also essential. Fundraising is also great training for asking for the order when it's time to approach customers. It's not all scary, though, and can even be exhilarating. Receiving that first investment check is one of the highest highs an entrepreneur will have, especially during the beginning stages of the startup. Look forward to that moment, and take action to get there as soon as you can. It will help you get the momentum (and confidence) you need to raise the next $999,999.

An Investor's Perspective
Randy Komisar, Kleiner Perkins Caufield Byers

Sometimes it's good to get an outside perspective. When putting together my thoughts for this book, which focuses on raising capital outside of Silicon Valley, I thought it would also be useful to include the opinion of somebody *inside* of Silicon Valley as well. And there are very few people whose backgrounds embody Silicon Valley as much as Randy Komisar's. Serving as a senior legal executive at Apple and CEO of LucasArts Entertainment, Randy has had the unique opportunity to learn from some of tech and entertainment's titans like Steve Jobs and George Lucas. He used that experience to help other companies, including WebTV, TiVO, and Nest, acting as either a "Virtual CEO" or Board Member. Currently, Randy is a Senior Partner at the venerable venture capital institution, Kleiner Perkins Caufield Byers. In his "spare time", he's managed to find a way to write two bestselling business books (*The Monk and the Riddle* and *Getting to Plan B*) and lectures on Entrepreneurship at Stanford University.

Randy freely admits that if a startup is looking for their first dollar from him, the company does need to be located in Silicon Valley, at least in the formative stage of the business.

"There's no doubt that there are smart people everywhere on the planet. But as a venture capitalist, I view my money as fungible. My time and attention, however, is not. As somebody who likes to work very closely with the entrepreneurs I invest in, my proximity is very important in the formative stages of the business. I want to make sure I can do everything possible to help the founders navigate their entrepreneurial journey, and the best way for me to do that is to be near them. I invest as much time in the entrepreneurs and their personal development as I do in the business. For later stage businesses that have been proven out, I can go farther afield. But I prefer to be very close to the early-stage startups that I invest in."

Knowing that, should everybody flock to Silicon Valley if they want to start their business? Randy's answer might surprise you.

"There's no place that has a monopoly on smart, creative innovators and entrepreneurs. There are certainly places that have been practicing the profession of entrepreneurship longer and have more resources to draw upon, and Silicon Valley is one of those places. But startup founders should really think about where their business would benefit most from when starting it. Where is the product's potential customer base? Where can you best compete for talent? Yes, there is money in Silicon Valley but people shouldn't move there just for the money. In many cases, getting started *outside* of Silicon Valley can actually buy you twice the amount of runway for the same amount of money. If you're able to build traction in that amount of time and end up with a very compelling book of evidence to prove to investors that you're on the right track, you'll have the luxury of being able to *choose* which group of investors and geographic location are right for your business."

Ultimately, though, where should that first dollar of investment come from? Does it make sense to try to convince venture capital institutions? Are Angel Investors a better fit for steed-stage investing?

"As an entrepreneur, it's important to find investors who can really help you along the way. They can come in the form of people who have direct experience in your specific industry, or with the critical assumptions and leaps of faith you're making with your business. Or, this could be the bell-cow in your industry that can open up doors that your business needs opened, whether to potential customers or other investors. Regardless, it's important that the earliest investors believe in *you* and are just as excited about your business as *you* are. Often times, institutional funds invest in seed-stage startups simply for option value. The venture capital firm is simply buying an option to invest more later on. For them, it's a relatively small price to pay just to see if the business can develop. They're not investing with the same kind of conviction that the entrepreneur has for the business. That's not to say that such an option-investment can't be helpful, but it is very different than an investment coming from a firm or individual with a strong conviction and belief in the entrepreneur."

12. INVESTMENT THAT DOESN'T DILUTE OWNERSHIP

Before you go on and continue to fill out your investment round, it's worth pausing to remember that you're going to have to give up something in order to get the investment. In this chapter, we'll briefly discuss the most common vehicles that you will likely encounter at this stage: equity and convertible debt.

With an equity investment, you are giving up shares in your company now in exchange for the investment that you receive.

With a convertible debt investment, you are essentially taking out a loan from an investor, however, instead of paying the money back, the loan balance will convert into equity at a future date.

There are several benefits of raising funds using a convertible note. Notably, the documents are relatively simple and straightforward, resulting in minimal legal costs when compared to a straight equity deal. Also, the founder is able to put off placing a numerical value on the business until a later date. If the entrepreneur makes great progress, this should result in an overall increase in the value of the company and means that the founder will not be giving up as much ownership when the loan is converted. Because of the extra risk taken on by the investors who buy convertible notes, the loan terms are often "sweetened" using warrants (low cost, fixed priced shares that can be paid for at a later date) or the promise of allowing the loan to convert into equity at a lower price the one paid by new investors.

On the other hand, many founders prefer raising funds through the sale of shares (equity) in the company, because it is completely clear what the investor is actually buying. This makes things as cut and dried as possible. Over the course of the past few years, accelerators and incubators like Y-Combinator have crafted standardized documents that they make available on their websites. This broad dissemination of previously secretive information has simplified the process of raising funds by educating both founder and investor. Using pre-drafted documents downloaded from a verified source on the web cuts down even further on legal costs. In this regard, more transparency has been great for entrepreneurs. A link to these documents can be found at SeedFundingBook.com/FreeResources.

Proponents of direct equity investments at the seed-stage argue that convertible notes actually don't put off the valuation discussion. While a direct valuation is not actually set, a valuation cap is sometimes used in a convertible note, meaning that the price per share cannot exceed a certain number upon conversion. By honing in on that number, there is essentially an implied value of the company.

Both arguments are valid, and which instrument is most appropriate in your situation is something to be negotiated between you and your investor. The best guidance I can give is to talk to multiple founders who have raised seed-stage capital using convertible notes and equity and ask about their experiences. For a primer on these investment vehicles along with all sorts of other "nuts and bolts" related to startup capital raising, consider reading the book "Venture Deals", by Brad Feld and Jason Mendelson. The book details all sorts of investment terminology and term sheet nuances that are important for founders to understand.

Funds that don't dilute your ownership

Not all of the capital you raise has to dilute your ownership. For instance, the first $60,000 raised for eFuneral wasn't completely dilutive. Two of these investments were convertible note investments. The other $20,000 raised was in the form of a grant that we didn't have to pay back.

Yes, that's right – a grant. Free money.

Believe it or not, there are lots of opportunities for startups, particularly those outside of entrepreneurial hotbeds like Silicon

Valley, to access grants and other forms of capital that don't dilute ownership in the company.

Startup grants provided by entrepreneurial nonprofits and foundations

While Silicon Valley doesn't need to rely on government funding in order to foster a thriving startup ecosystem, many burgeoning startup communities often need a nudge in order to get started, and they look to government and foundation funding for that boost. There are often grants and startup-friendly loans offered by these groups to startups at even very early stages. Receiving funding from these sources can be even more valuable beyond the actual capital received. It can be an important validation to other investors who are considering making an investment in your startup as well. The disadvantage of raising funds through these sources is, in certain instances, a lengthy and cumbersome process, sometimes necessitating the creation of robust business plans, detailed financials, and several rounds of pitching. That process can sometimes distract you from running your business. However, even if it's somewhat time consuming, going through the process set up by these entities will better prepare you for future investment conversations. Before deciding to start any of these more formalized processes, make sure the "size of the prize" is commensurate with the time you'll have to spend jumping through their hoops.

Startup Loans

Similar to entrepreneurial nonprofits and foundations, up and coming startup communities are starting to see financial lenders offer specific financial products that are geared towards startup founders. It's typically not the traditional institutions that offer these products to founders, so look beyond your neighborhood banks. In fact, many startup-focused micro-lending programs such as KIVA and others have become available online. In these cases, you can borrow a certain amount from a number of people. Instead of asking for $10,000 from one person you can receive $10 from 1,000 different people. Keep in mind, however, that these loans are often personal in nature, meaning that you are individually on the hook for paying the money back.

Receiving investment from your customers

Some startups are in the position to have their customers finance their business. Some even allow customers to transfer this financing into an equity stake. This is an interesting approach and is likely to intrigue other investors. After all, if customers are so impressed with your business that they're willing to invest in it, you must be onto something.

Rather than asking your customers to invest in a typical manner, form the "investment" in a way of an advance purchase. No matter what your business is, you could approach customers and ask them to pay up front in advance of receiving future products or services. In exchange, you can offer them a deeper discount than you'd offer other customers. You could even make this advance contingent on certain deliverables, too (i.e. upon the release of your product, upon your company raising a certain amount of capital, etc). The advantages to the customer include getting early access to your product ahead of the competition, and, of course, receiving a deep price discount. It's almost guaranteed that other investors will be impressed that customers are already making a financial bet on your company, and you've gotten to this point without having to give up any ownership.

Approach the Crowds

Startup founders from all parts of the world have begun approaching the masses through the use of crowdfunding. Crowdfunding platforms such as Kickstarter, IndieGoGo, and Fundable allow entrepreneurs to list "projects" for which they're seeking funding, like launching a new app, building a product, or offering a new service. These platforms allow the founders to invite others to make a financial contribution to the project. Through these platforms, an individual typically describes the project in detail, and creates a compelling video that showcases a demo or early prototype. In many cases, individuals make "donations" and receive gifts in exchange for their donation. However, these donations aren't altogether altruistic. Usually, the gift received is the new product or service, or something else of value related to the product or service. For instance, a Kickstarter campaign for the first Pebble Watch saw over $10 Million in donations raised and those that contributed were the first to receive the actual product. It's newer Pebble Time smartwatch eclipsed that total in 2015 within just a couple of days, and at the publishing of this book, became the most funded Kickstarter project ever. In a sense, this platform acts as a way for early adopters to pre-order. Crowdfunding can be tricky, though, and certainly isn't an easy way to raise $1 million overnight. Often, some track record of previous success, a slick demo video, and a little luck in generating good PR are all ingredients for successful crowdfunding campaigns. However, since over $1 Billion in funds have been raised through crowdfunding – this approach is becoming more and more viable.

Hustle on the side

Many founders opt for raising money in ways that are unrelated to their business at all. Instead of asking for money from investors, some founders choose to leverage other skills that they have to freelance on the side and use *that* money to invest into their startup business. When you do this, you are your own investor and you don't have to worry about giving up ownership to anybody else. In fact, you could technically keep doing this until you have enough funds to launch and then use customer dollars to continue to fuel your business. AirBnB is famed for needing money to launch their business, and came up with the idea to sell "Obama O's" cereal during the height of the 2008 presidential election in order to raise money to launch. The result? They sold over $100,000 worth of cereal, and they invested that money directly back into their business. You don't have to create a presidential line of cereal. But you could take on side projects, no matter how small, to start chipping away at your fundraise goal piece by piece.

The Big Takeaway

Raising money for your startup doesn't always have to come in the form of traditional investment. In fact, investors often respect founders who "hustle" to bring in capital any way that they can in the beginning without giving up any equity. Give thought to what's best for your type of business, whether it's applying for local grants, launching a crowdfunding campaign, or taking on side projects in order to earn money without having to give up any equity.

An Entrepreneur's Perspective
Tanisha Robinson, Print Syndicate

As the elevator doors open into the downtown Columbus, Ohio offices of Print Syndicate, it only takes a few steps to realize that you're walking into a space of a company that has recently either gone through a major round of layoffs, or is poised for explosive growth. There's lots of room in the modern, yet industrial, open layout office, which includes empty workstations and barren rooms. But after further review, it is apparent that there's also a magical spark seen in the eyes of the passionate designers, developers, and other team members who are actively engaged in front of their workstations. It's clear that Print Syndicate, which creates trendy apparel and other products on-demand through its Merica Made, Activate Apparel and Look Human brands, isn't a falling star. It's a rocket ship, and Tanisha Robinson, Co-Founder and CEO, can be considered the captain.

Tanisha's story of how she and her co-founder started the company is different than the usual stories of founders raising large seed rounds and using that money to turn their good idea into a business. In fact, Tanisha and her team didn't seek any outside funding in the beginning.

"This isn't my first startup. The idea of building a business isn't new to me. But one thing I've learned is that the best way to get funding is to first build a valuable company. Because of this, we wanted to build something that people actually *wanted* to invest in instead of spending so much time trying to convince investors that we could actually build a business. In our case, we figured out the right model for our business before ever taking any investment at all. We generated revenue immediately and were profitable from the beginning."

This bootstrapping approach worked quite well for Print Syndicate. Without taking a dime from investors, they were able to create the type of high-growth environment that most founders would envy. Yet, later on, Tanisha and her team did decide to bring investors on board. But they weren't interested in just any investors. Print Syndicate's first round of funding – over $4 Million – came from investors who had previously started companies like Groupon, Zappos, and Shoebuy. This was no coincidence.

"We were growing so fast, but there was stuff that was happening that we just hadn't seen before. We didn't necessarily *need* money. We needed insight. We were starting to build relationships with people from the Zappos team and that helped a lot. But it made us realize that if we were tied even closer together, it could help even more. That's when we decided to raise our first big round of funding, specifically from people who have walked in our shoes."

With the intense growth that Print Syndicate is experiencing coupled with its influx of cash from major out-of-town investors, it wouldn't be surprising to see a similar business with the same success moving its location outside of Columbus to be either closer to its investors or the industry's major players. Don't expect to see that happen anytime soon, though.

"This is a Columbus story. We want the success we're experiencing to spread throughout Columbus. And if we're really successful in the long run, we want that success to stay in Columbus. We could take our business anywhere. But what's the point? We belong here."

13. MULTIPLY YOUR MONEY

Even though the first dollar of investment is the hardest to raise, it doesn't mean that the rest is a cakewalk. However, it's critical that you move swiftly once that first dollar is in, as the likelihood of you adding onto that investment begins to diminish with each day that passes. Once your first investor hands over the check and you take it to the bank to see the bump in the balance of your account, it's time to ramp up your efforts.

Keep others informed

For many new startups, it's common that the first time they make their presence known online is through a landing page. As discussed in Chapter Two, Drew Houston first launched DropBox with a simple landing page that included a video demo and a place to sign up to receive more information about the startup. While I'm not recommending that you build a landing page to communicate with *investors*, I do recommend that you follow the same logic and begin to build up a list of potential investors with whom you will communicate progress, even during these beginning stages. Especially once you've accepted your first outside investment, it's important to let other potential investors who have expressed an interest in your startup know about your funding and product progress.

There are a few tools out there to help you build this list:

WordPress

At this point, you should already have a list of investors with whom you're in regular communication. Wordpress is one tool that you can use, as it allows anybody (even non-developers) to create a simple website or blog in a relatively short period of time. One key feature with WordPress is that it allows for very specific privacy features. You can restrict access so that only those with a username or password are given access, in effect creating a private blog. You can even set the blog up to automatically send emails to your mailing list as soon as you make a post, alleviating the need for investors to remember to visit the website. We took this approach with eFuneral, and it worked incredibly well. This created a central place that investors could go to if they ever needed to check on our progress and was automated enough to keep all investors informed, especially those who rarely visited the private blog.

Simple CRM tool (or Google Drive)

Aside from sharing information with your investors, having a central repository for you to keep track of all of the information you shared can be useful. If communications were only limited to your private blog, then you wouldn't need much else to manage this. But most of the time, those updates will lead to additional emails, phone calls, and meetings. Very basic CRM programs offered through Google Apps or other platforms can help you keep track of all of the communications you have with investors. It's helpful to track this in a single place so you can stay organized, remember with whom you spoke with, the time and date of the conversations, and exactly what you said. Google Apps offers certain paid and free CRM tools. You can also simply use Google Drive to create a basic spreadsheet and manage it in a similar way.

Regardless of how you're keeping potential investors informed, just remember that the first time they hear from you shouldn't be a direct ask for investment. Building a potential investor list and starting regular communication with those potential investors should be one of the first things you do after reading this book (or, perhaps, *right now!*) Regardless of how you do it, be sure to let your list of potential investors know once you have your first investor. This can be great motivation for those other individuals to act quickly.

Ask for a referral

Like in sales, referrals are also great way for the first dollar of investment to quickly lead to another from somebody else. When you have an investor who already believes in you so much that they're investing their own money, it's perfectly acceptable to ask them if they know of any other like-minded people who might be interested in doing the same. A referral in this scenario does several things:

The person you're being referred to knows up front that they're not the *first* investor in this deal. This is important, because as we already discussed – most investors don't like writing the very first investment check a startup takes in.

This referral can cause a bit of positive peer pressure. Investors can be influenced by the other investors with whom they're closely connected. If it's good enough for their friend that referred you, why shouldn't the person you're being referred to invest?

Referrals help demonstrate social proof. To go along with both above points, most investors want to know that you've been validated somehow. Social proof is the validation that one receives by having respected individuals heavily involved in your venture, whether they're involved as key employees or investors.

Silicon Valley can seem like a tightknit community to founders and investors, but the same is true for startup communities outside of Silicon Valley. In these places, investors likely have a much lower risk tolerance, which makes it important for them to know that you've been properly vetted. Referrals help show that somebody else has already done enough research on you to determine that you have a business worth investing in.

Be open to road trips

A mistake that many first-time founders outside of Silicon Valley make is that they believe they are confined to raising capital in the startup community where they live. It's important to look beyond your local community. While it's true that many investors prefer to invest in companies located near them – especially at the seed stage – there are other investors who firmly believe that a company worth investing knows no bounds. An exciting opportunity located in Tampa should be just as fundable as an exciting company located in Silicon Valley.

To get a sense of what other startup communities are like and to help you expand your network, plan short stops in other startup communities (even Silicon Valley itself) and make it a point to reach out to other startups and investors in the area. Often times, these founders are curious about other startups outside of their hometown and will be very receptive to meeting. If you can only get one meeting, ask that individual who else you should meet with while you're there or on your next visit. One meeting can quickly lead to three or four. This may even lead to meeting an investor you would never have met any other way. Even nothing else, it will help you build up connections outside of your local area that may come in handy at some future date.

While it's a good idea to reach out in advance to pre-arrange meetings, I've found that some of my most productive visits to certain startup communities happened when things weren't so planned out in advance. Rather than waiting to secure several meetings before booking a trip to Silicon Valley, I decided to simply book the trip and promised myself I'd find a way to set up the meetings I was looking for. Most of my meetings were confirmed either while I was mid-air on my way to California or when I was already in town.

Short on money to plan such trips? It's not an excuse. You can start by visiting other startup communities within driving distance of where you're located. And if you do want to plan a multi-day trip, couchsurfing and AirBnB are great options to find places to stay on the cheap.

The Big Takeaway

Your networking activities should begin to ramp up after you've accepted your first investment; it's the best time to strike. Many investors don't like to be the lead investor in a startup (despite what they might tell you). For those that seem legitimately interested in your startup, yet don't want to make the first investment, it's time to get back in front of them.

An Entrepreneur's Perspective
Alex Frommeyer, Beam Technologies

When people think of areas ripe for innovation – especially within the "quantified self" movement that has been gaining steam – dental care is likely not the first that comes to mind. But Alex Frommeyer and his two co-founders thought differently. They weren't turned off or bored by dental care. They saw an opportunity within it. It shouldn't come as a big surprise, though. Alex and his team spent a significant amount of time learning about technology within the dental care market after working on a consulting project for a client in the field. What they didn't realize at the time, however, was that they would go on to launch dental care products that would attract millions of dollars in venture capital investment and be touted nationally by the likes of Wall Street Journal, Forbes, and others.

Prior to all of the attention from venture capitalists and media moguls, Alex and his partners found themselves in the NuLu district of Louisville, Kentucky. It was here where they created their first product: "The Beam Brush" – a manual toothbrush with an embedded sensor that communicates with an iOS or Android app to help users understand their oral care habits – and found their initial investors. Perhaps not surprisingly, some of the first investment checks Alex collected were from Louisville-based investors.

"In a place like Louisville, people can really roll out the red carpet for entrepreneurs. People want to see success stories coming from the region, and they're much more likely to find a way to help you somehow. The area may still be nascent as a startup/investment community, but we certainly benefited from having one of the more interesting stories to tell as entrepreneurs. We were able to use some of that early momentum to find our first investors, many of whom happened to be local."

Like many other companies located outside of traditional startup communities – the team at Beam Technologies found that, while they were able to attract some investment locally, Louisville was not likely to be able to provide them with the entire amount of capital they needed. So they started to keep their eyes open for investors outside of their local community.

Enter Drive Capital.

The upstart Ohio-based venture capital group founded by former partners from Sequoia Capital invested $5 million into Beam Technologies. Of course, the connection didn't just happen on its own. Alex and his team, and even the city of Louisville, all had a role in building the relationship.

"We actually met some of the members of the Drive Capital team at the Kentucky Derby. The local Chamber of Commerce had invited them to Kentucky to not only enjoy the derby, but also to meet some of the interesting technology companies in the area. Over the course of the weekend, we made it a point to get to know them and make sure that they left knowing who we were. We were beginning to think of ways that we could network with different investors outside of our local area, and here we were, getting to know one of the biggest investors in the Midwest, all without having to leave our own city."

Had Alex not focused at all on meeting and getting to know investors *outside* of his local community, would he have been able to raise the same amount of capital purely from his local startup community? Maybe, but probably not. Regardless, the $5 million investment that Beam Technologies received will allow the team to focus on creating new, innovative physical and digital products – and they don't need to worry about what might have happened if they didn't keep an open mind as to where their investment would come from.

14. CLOSE THE ROUND

By now, you've learned how to adequately prepare yourself for the *process* of raising startup capital while operating outside of Silicon Valley, you've done the important legwork of targeting the right kind of investors, and have even started to bring some of those investors on board.

It's time to close out the round. Or is it?

It's easy for first-time startup founders to get caught up talking about funding rounds – both in terms of size, and the concept itself. But let's face it. Outside of Silicon Valley, the concept of a $1 million seed round closing in less than a week after a hastily launched AngelList profile just isn't realistic for most startups. When you read articles on TechCrunch, you may believe that this is how things actually work. But it's not reality for the "rest of us." Just because there aren't many overnight $1 million seed rounds outside of Silicon Valley doesn't mean that you can't strategically plan for – and close – the funding you need to get your business started.

When considering a specific target amount to raise in a seed round, ask yourself what milestones you're striving to achieve and determine how much it will cost to reach each one. If you're trying to raise $250,000 be prepared to answer the question, "Why that number? Why isn't it $500,000? Why isn't it $1 Million? What about $100,000?" Setting an arbitrary size to your seed round – and also giving yourself a fixed timeframe in which to raise it – isn't helpful. Instead, ask yourself the following questions:

What proof you need to show whether your business model works?

How much time will it take before your startup begins to earn revenue, or even actively recruit users?

How long do you think it will take before your business can generate enough revenue each month to cover expenses (i.e. how long will it take until you get to breakeven?)

What are the essential milestones that you need to achieve in order to show others that your startup has value?

Set clear milestones to determine the size and stage of your round.

Rather than using a nice, round general figure – such as $1 Million or $500,000 as your funding goal, work backwards to calculate how much you actually *need* to achieve your business's important milestones. These milestones should be set for two reasons. First, they will act as clear goalposts for you to measure whether you're actually achieving the traction you anticipated. Second, each milestone is a "proof point" for investors, showing them intermediate results that allow them to determine whether or not to continue investing.

After you've determined what these milestones are, you can then work backwards and determine the expenses you'll incur to get to each one. As you formulate your proposed budget, keep in mind that you don't need to construct unnecessary barriers by limiting the timeframe in which you're willing to raise your seed round. It might be true that $1 Million will enable you to enjoy 24 months of runway and get you to a point where you can start earning enough revenue to have proven out your business model. But if you can't raise $1 Million all at once, consider whether there's a way to break the budget down into smaller phases. Being able to raise $250,000 now – and another $250,000 each time you achieve a goal might be more manageable way to go. You also may be able to negotiate better terms for each successive inflow of capital, as you will have more positive proof at each juncture to show that you are on the right track.

Set meaningful deadlines as to why you need funding *right now*.

Milestones can help you articulate why you need the funding you're asking for. Meaningful deadlines can help you articulate why you need that funding *now*. Use time-sensitive events to set meaningful deadlines with your investors in order to encourage them to invest now instead of waiting. Is there an important industry conference that you're aiming to attend with a completed product? Do you need to onboard another developer and designer in order to launch your product in time to coincide with your customers' buying cycles? These are the type of events that can translate into fundraising deadlines for you – and can help in creating some motivation for investors to come in now as opposed to waiting.

A word of caution on deadlines: If they're not meaningful, or if you don't stick to them, you run the risk of losing some credibility in your investors' eyes. For instance, if you tell them that you need to raise funding by April in order to have your product ready for the industry's annual conference – you had better not come back to them in June with the same message. Of course, this doesn't mean you can't approach them again after your deadline has passed. But you should be prepared to discuss the ramifications of missing the important deadline that you previously communicated with them.

Make it your full time job.

All of the activities discussed until this chapter can be done "on the side" while you're doing other important things to help build your business. But if you're serious about closing your first round of investment, there will come a time when you – or somebody on your team – will need to focus on this task full-time. Think of all of the activities up until now as fireworks – exciting and interesting, but something that doesn't need your full focus. Now, we're onto the grand finale. This requires your full, dedicated attention.

During this period, your day should be filled with sending emails and making phone calls asking for referrals, scheduling coffee meetings with potential investors, and researching who to have your next conversations with. Treat managing your pipeline of potential investors the same way that you would a pipeline of customers. As we discussed in the previous chapter, a simple CRM tool or Google Drive can help you manage your communications with investors and allow you to understand where they are in your pipeline. Hopefully, these aren't brand new conversations at this stage, as you should have already worked to build a pipeline of potential investors and have been keeping them informed.

If all of this sounds scary to you, it's time to overcome any fears you have. You'll experience rejection in this phase. In fact, you're likely to hear "No" ten times (or more) for each time you hear "Yes" from investors at this stage. But it only takes one investor to say "Yes" to get your startup funded.

Don't overthink things, but trust your gut.

If you're lucky enough to have captured the attention of investors and are on the verge of closing your seed round you must not let the little things get in the way of getting a deal done. It is at this stage where first-time founders generally run into issues that, while they seem important, are really just a lot of noise.

Valuation is at the top of the list of noisy items. At first glance, this would seem to be an ultra-important factor in negotiations. First time founders sometimes believe it is the *most important* factor. While it's certainly not an area to be overlooked, a "winning" valuation negotiation is rarely singled out as the most critical success factor for any new startup. However, founders *have* attributed at least a portion of their success to the quality of their initial investors. Don't let valuation be the factor that you're trying to optimize for at this stage. Instead, focus on bringing on the right kind of investors at a fair valuation.

What is a fair valuation? Like consumer products and services, the market sets valuation. The value of your startup is whatever an investor is willing to pay. For startups outside of Silicon Valley, the unfortunate truth is that the market usually dictates a lower valuation than if those startups happened to be located in Silicon Valley. You can get a sense of current market terms by using tools like AngelList or, even better, by simply networking with founders in the geographies where you're raising money. While you don't want to let valuation be the primary factor behind why a deal happens or falls apart, it is important to consider all of the terms of a deal before moving forward with an investor:

Does the investor require a Board seat? What voting or veto rights is the investor asking for? If your company were to sell sometime down the road, how much would you need to pay your investor before you start to earn anything from a sale? Does your investor require you to set aside a certain number of shares to allocate for an Employee Options Pool?

These can all be very confusing issues to consider. Because of this, it's important to have a close network of mentors who have gone through the experience of taking in capital, along with a reputable business attorney who has deep experience in helping startups raise capital.

In the end, though, nobody – not your mentors nor your attorney – can *tell* you what to do. That call will be yours to make. And if a deal simply doesn't feel right to you, you have to trust yourself enough to be able to walk away. Even if it means that there's no guarantee you'll see another offer in the future.

The Big Takeaway

It's time to close your round and move on to starting your business. But rather than focusing on a big, round number and an arbitrary timeframe in which to close your round, set clear milestones and communicate your rationale for why you need the amount you're asking for. Since you've worked hard to get to this point, be sure to dedicate the time and energy that's required to successfully close your round; don't let the little things get in the way of getting a deal done. Engage your network and trust your gut when you're evaluating whether or not a deal makes sense for you.

An Entrepreneur's Perspective
Danielle Morrill, Mattermark

Danielle Morrill has placed herself squarely in the center of the startup universe. It's not just that she lives in San Francisco. As the Co-Founder and CEO of Mattermark, a startup that helps venture capital firms, business development professionals and others to research, track and monitor over one million different private companies, Danielle has built a platform that gives her a unique vantage point over the entire global startup landscape. Of course, Danielle doesn't just monitor startups. She's *lived* them. Danielle served as an early employee for two Seattle-based startups, including the popular cloud communications technology provider, Twilio. In 2012, Danielle decided to take the leap and began to transition from "early employee" to "Founder" when she was accepted into Y-Combinator's cohort.

Throughout her various startup experiences, Danielle and her co-founders have raised millions of dollars in startup seed capital from some of the biggest and well-known investors both inside and outside of Silicon Valley. For entrepreneurs going through the same process, Danielle's first piece of advice is to get comfortable with asking for money.

"It can be hard to ask for money, especially for people who haven't done it before. But at the end of the day, you *actually* have to ask. Some conversations with investors start as legitimate feedback sessions, and that's great. But soon enough, you have to *ask* an investor to invest. I've found that the best way to practice is to just throw yourself into the fire and increase the volume of investor meetings you're taking. The first couple of investor meetings could be uncomfortable, but by the time you've reached your 50th or 100th conversation, that discomfort will no longer exist."

Danielle recognizes that founders can feel the pressure to keep things moving along with their investors. On actually getting to a closing, Danielle reminds founders that you don't have to close the entire round all at once.

"At the end of the day, you're raising money because you need that money in the bank now. If you have one investor who is ready to invest – but they only represent 5% of the total round you're trying to raise – remember that you don't need to wait to close *everybody* before you close that particular investor. Get that money in the bank now. It's completely acceptable to close on a rolling basis. Some investors may be opposed to this, but if you set this precedent early, you may be able to close your entire round on a rolling basis."

Danielle realizes that investors can be tricky. Even those that seem very interested in investing can sometimes take a bit too long to make a decision. For those "tough to convince" investors, prepare to be bold.

"When an investor is on the fence and is considering investing "later" as opposed to right now, be blunt with them. Tell them that you can't guarantee that there will be room for them in the future - the opportunity for them is *right now*. In the end, if the investor is really not all that sure about you and your business, and chooses to wait, you probably don't want them as an investor anyway. Focus on the investors that are so excited about you and your startup that they're asking you how *soon* they can invest – not how long they can wait. Yes, approaching investors this way is risky. But they'll respect you for it."

15. A FEW FINAL WORDS

The notion of needing to move to Silicon Valley or another venture capital hotspot to raise the funding you need to get your startup off the ground and launched is completely and utterly flawed. It's just not true. I personally can attest to this and so can thousands of other founders located in places *outside* of San Francisco, Silicon Valley and other major startup hubs.

It's true that there are unique challenges that first-time founders face outside of Silicon Valley:

Your startup community may not be flooded with stories of successful startups that have generated significant financial returns for their investors.

That's okay. It means your startup can be the next big success story in your community. And, let's face it, in these up-and-coming startup communities; everybody is looking for success stories. Founders and investors hope that the next Tumblr, SnapChat, or Twitter can come from *their* startup community.

Your startup community may not have a deep network of angel investors willing to bet on the high-risk world of early stage technology investing.

This is a challenge, but it's not one that can't be overcome. Even if your startup community doesn't have investors with household names, there likely are investors with deep pockets. You just have to find them. They may not know your industry very well, but they're not only investing in your business. They're investing in you. Don't forget that you don't have to be confined to your own local area, either. Branch out. Take a roadtrip. You may be surprised by what you find.

You might not be connected to other startup founders who face similar challenges – or to those who have "been there and done that" before.

This is an easy one. *Get* connected. Go make your own connections. Send a cold email to a local founder. Volunteer at local startup events. Start your own startup-oriented meetups. There's no (good) excuse for not proactively building your own network. In fact, peer mentoring can be a very powerful thing for first-time founders. After all, who else can relate to what you're going through?

Unfortunately, reading this book won't necessarily make the process of raising $1 million for your startup venture a walk in the park. I wish that were the case. However, I'm hopeful that this has given you an inside peek at what it really takes to successfully raise a seed round for your decidedly non-Valley startup. What I can guarantee is that the insights from this book will help you put yourself on a faster track to finding the funding you need – whether you're inside or outside of Silicon Valley.

EPILOGUE (THE REST OF MY STORY)

There I was, sitting in the parking lot of the Agora Theater. I was stalling for a meeting that I simply didn't want to have. The Agora Theater was one of Cleveland's most well-known historical entertainment venues with roots dating back to 1913. Now, the Agora Theater also houses a dozen or so startup companies in some renovated office space next to the auditorium. My company, eFuneral, was one of startups to call the Agora Theater home. We shared an airy, exposed-brick warehouse space with another startup company. It was a perfect fit for our six-person team. Cleveland might not have a lot the same type of hip workplaces you would find in San Francisco or Menlo Park. The Agora was one of the few locations that had this vibe.

Yet, I couldn't get myself to open the car door and enter the building because I knew that the moment I walked inside, the company that I helped build would change dramatically... for the worse. I had to let my entire team go, and I was sick about it. But there was no more stalling. I knew what I had to do, and so I began the slow march from the parking lot to the office.

Rewind to the 10xelerator

Starting with our drive down I-71 to Columbus, the summer of 2011 was a special time for Bryan and me. We had left our wives behind in order to dedicate ourselves fully to getting the business off the ground. Bryan and I set out to become known as the hardest working startup team at the 10xelerator, and we accomplished that. Early each morning, we would go into the loft-style workspace that the 10xelerator provided and would spend the next 8-10 hours focused on our business. Around 6pm, we would venture back to the house where we were living to quickly eat, and then park ourselves in the living room and work more until we couldn't keep our eyes open. Bryan was focused on designing and coding the early Beta version of the product while I focused on building relationships with potential customers and investors. We took advantage of every resource that the 10xelerator made available and started building amazing relationships with new mentors. By the end of our time at 10xelerator, Bryan and I felt like we were in a great place.

The funding started to come shortly thereafter. It helped that one of the mentors we were matched with was Doug Weintraub, a prominent Akron, Ohio-based angel investor. After meeting with Doug several times over the summer to brainstorm and seek counsel, in August he asked us a question we weren't expecting to hear, "Okay guys, when are you going to ask me to write a check?" We finally did ask and he wrote a sizable investment check. On the 10xelerator's Showcase Day, we met a representative from Flywheel Ventures, an early stage venture capital fund from Albuquerque, New Mexico. They were impressed with our pitch and made an effort to get to know us better in the weeks following Showcase Day. Ultimately, Flywheel Ventures decided to invest a small amount in our seed round. By the time we left the 10xelerator, we had circled nearly $400,000 from our mentors, these new investors, and other friends and family members we had pitched our company to.

When we came back to Cleveland, we discovered all of the funding sources that were available through government and foundation programs. These programs offered grants and startup-friendly low-interest loans for as much as $125,000. The funding for these programs was provided by the State of Ohio. The State of Ohio funds these programs to help spur economic development and continued investment in startup companies, encouraging entrepreneurs like Bryan and me to take the leap and start job creating, technology-oriented businesses. The downside of these various programs was that each had a very long application cycle, and required a lot of time and preparation. Yet, knowing that this capital was available, we started to go through these processes, which ultimately led to us obtaining over $250,000 in additional funding.

Building our company

Most of our focus when we returned to Cleveland wasn't actually on funding. We now had to actually build a *company*. With the initial $400,000 we were able to access, we recruited eFuneral's first two full-time employees: Leah Yomtovian Roush and Marko Zlatic. They both joined the team within three months after our move back from Columbus. While Leah's focus was on driving demand from users and Marko's was to help build out our funeral home network, they both understood that being in a startup meant that their job descriptions would likely evolve over time. They were more than willing to accept the challenge, and made great first-hires for eFuneral.

Things became a bit more complex right after we opened our office in Cleveland. Soon after we brought Marko and Leah on board, I got the news from my wife that she was pregnant with our first child. Six weeks later, Bryan learned that his wife was pregnant with their first child. Six weeks after that, Leah learned that she was pregnant with *her* first child. Three new babies on the way certainly compounded our personal and professional responsibilities. Yet we had no choice, we knew that we simply had to put as much into eFuneral as we possibly could so that it could provide for all of our families.

Launching and learning

In February of 2012, everything we had been working towards finally came to a head. We were ready to launch. Up until this point, Bryan was finishing his work building the beta version of eFuneral while Marko, Leah, and I were working on all sorts of pre-launch activities. Most notably, we signed up nearly 30% of the funeral home locations throughout Greater Cleveland to be in our network. Our initial business model was relatively simple. Funeral homes could sign up to be in our network for free. Families could then submit an inquiry on eFuneral.com indicating what they were looking for in a funeral service. The funeral homes in our network then had an opportunity to respond with a quote. The family could review the quotes, along with ratings and reviews that might exist for those funeral homes, and choose to work with whichever funeral home they believed was the best fit for them. The funeral home paid us a success fee only after a family chose to work with them.

Funeral homes were skeptical about us from the beginning. There really hadn't been many technology businesses to sprout up within their industry. In fact, some funeral home owners claimed that the Internet had no place in their business at all. Many funeral home owners even refused to set up websites. Still, we were able to find many funeral homes that were willing to give us a shot, especially because there really wasn't much risk in signing up.

Our product worked, technically. Before long, anytime somebody would submit an inquiry on eFuneral, they would receive between 5-7 quotes from area funeral homes within just a few minutes. Before eFuneral, this simply wasn't possible. It would take hours, if not days, to accumulate that number of funeral home quotes. However, the *business model* wasn't working for us. Most of the inquiries submitted through the eFuneral website were actually by people planning their funeral years in advance. Funeral Directors did like hearing from these families, but our business wasn't set up very well to generate revenue from these types of inquiries.

After several months, we were starting to generate some revenue, but we were learning first-hand that there were severe flaws with our initial business model. Yet, all hope was not lost. Our biggest supporters came from the hospice community. We learned that hospice serves nearly 60% of individuals at the very end of their life. And we learned that, often times, these individuals made no funeral plans at all, leaving their families to struggle the same way that my family struggled when my cousin, Ed, died. The hospice professionals we were meeting with were very encouraging about our business and thought it was something that was needed, but they stopped short of recommending it to their patients since we didn't have information available for the majority of funeral homes in their general area. We knew that some type of pivot was necessary - one that would include a better business model, but would also see to it that hospice facilities *would* be willing to recommend eFuneral to families.

Another push for funding

Changing course, however, meant that we'd need additional technical resources to work with Bryan to build and evolve our product. We didn't have money in the budget for adding headcount at this stage, so we decided to raise additional funding on top of we had already raised. Despite being in the middle of a pivot, we were able to find a couple of angel investors and an institutional funding source, JumpStart, to invest another $300,000 into our business. With those funds, we were able to recruit Rob Adams, a very talented software engineer, to supplement the product development work that Bryan was doing.

The pivot(s)

We began changing the pieces of the business that we felt were holding us back from generating revenue and earning the recommendations of hospice, a group that we felt strongly would help in building our user base. Rather than only provide information for those funeral homes that had signed up to be in our network, we went out and collected certain pieces of information for *all* of the funeral homes in Greater Cleveland. This included pricing information that we personally collected from each individual funeral home, pictures of funeral homes available on Google Maps, and reviews for any funeral homes that existed on platforms like Yelp or Google. We assembled all of this information and made it available in our funeral home profiles. Funeral homes that were in our network could add other features that would make them stand out. They would also be featured more prominently than non-members. Our belief was that this approach would enable hospice to recommend eFuneral to their clients, thus driving users to our website and enabling us to generate more revenue.

A part of our pivot strategy worked really well. Hospice was more willing to recommend us. In fact, so many hospice organizations were interested in our services that we brought Chelsea Gumucio onto our team – a part-time licensed social worker with hospice experience – to help us foster these relationships.

Unfortunately, another part of the pivot failed in a big way. By providing the pricing information for each funeral home, families no longer felt the need to submit an inquiry to receive a custom quote. They felt that they had the all of the information they needed once they saw the pricing information we provided to them directly in the funeral home's profile. This helped them, but it really hurt us because we now had no way of knowing which families we were specifically helping and which were choosing to work with funeral homes in our network.

We continued to iterate our model twice more in an effort to really prove out eFuneral as a money-making business. We created a very useful service that actually helped people during one of the most difficult times in their life. However, despite generating *some* revenue, we still hadn't proven out that eFuneral could be a truly viable company.

The decision

In the summer of 2013, just two years after Bryan and I decided to take the leap, we were faced with an incredibly difficult decision. Our runway was coming to an end. We knew by the end of the year, there would be no more cash in the bank to sustain the business. Unfortunately, revenue wasn't strong enough to keep the business sustained at this point either. We were faced with four options:

Raise money from our current investors.

This was a real possibility. All of our investors knew the state of the business, as we made it a point to keep both our investors and employees very informed throughout the ups and downs of eFuneral. We felt that we owed them that type of transparency. Despite being at this difficult stage, certain investors came to us and said that they would be willing to invest a little more into the business, but *only* if I personally felt we were turning the corner as a business. With these funds, we would probably be able to create a few more months of runway.

Raise money from new investors.

Actually, all along, we had planning to raise money from new investors and current investors at this stage. We just expected to be in a better place with regard to proving out our business model. We intended to pitch new investors at this stage on the notion that we've proven the business out and just needed more funding to scale. But I obviously couldn't deliver that message anymore. My pitch would have to be much different if we decided to go this route.

Find an acquirer.

There were larger companies within the death care industry that we had been building relationships with. Some of these companies were intrigued by us, but were unsure how to really partner. They wanted to build an Internet presence, but weren't quite sure how. We knew that if we approached any of these companies about an acquisition at this stage, we weren't likely to get a deal done that would bring a big, if any, financial return to our investors or us. But it could be a viable way to keep some of what we built alive and possibly return *something* back to investors.

Wind the company down.

This was considered a last resort and would only be done if options #1, #2, and #3 weren't possible.

I knew in my heart that we simply couldn't raise money from our current investors. The funding they would provide was only there if I personally could assure them that we were truly turning a corner. The problem is that we weren't. If I took their money, we would simply be trying more things. While I could have easily accessed this money and bought a few months of additional runway, I knew that this wasn't the right thing to do.

Instead, I directed my efforts towards option #2 – having conversations with the new investors I had planned to pitch. Of course, my story had to change. I could no longer tell a story about how we'd proven our business model and now just needed funding to scale up.

Instead, I had to admit that we hadn't proven anything definitive. But I stressed that *nobody* had proven out an Internet-based funeral marketplace business like we'd built. If anybody had a head start at this, it was us. The venture capital groups that we spoke with were intrigued, but ultimately we simply hadn't achieved enough traction to warrant serious consideration from these groups.

With this option all but closed to us, our efforts turned to trying to find a company that might buy us. I presented our Board of Advisors with a list of 20 potential acquirers with many of which we'd already developed some sort of relationship or rapport. The Board agreed that we should begin to pursue these companies aggressively, but pointed out that in order to really give us the opportunity to complete a transaction, we would need much more runway than we had. If we were serious about trying to find an acquirer, we would need to cut every single expense we had. Bryan and I talked afterwards and realized that they were right. If we were going to pursue an acquisition, we would have to pare our team back down to just Bryan and me and focus solely on completing the type of sale – an asset sale – that these acquirers would be interested in.

The rest of the story

Having to face each one of our team members and let them go was one of the toughest things I have ever had to do. I braved my way into the office and asked everybody if we could meet up in one of our breakout rooms. It was there where I told them that this was the meeting that I never wanted to have. I went on to explain the situation to them and informed them that we'd continue to pay them for a few more weeks, but essentially their time at eFuneral was done. Bryan and I would do everything we could to help them find jobs, but we would now be focused on finding an acquirer for eFuneral.

Most situations like this might have turned ugly. Perhaps there would be arguments, with people storming out of the office. That wasn't the case for us. Instead, we all decided that the best way to end was to go to lunch together as a team and talk about all of the good times that we had. We laughed together. We shared all sorts of stories with each other about our trials and tribulations from the past 2+ years seedfundingbook.com/freeresources

– and there were plenty to share. This positive experience was only possible because of how transparent we were with our team about the struggles that we had. Even with that silver lining, though, it was still tough. As much as we laughed together that day, I certainly spent time crying later that evening.

Ultimately, Bryan and I did find a company that would go on to acquire eFuneral's assets. Homesteaders Life Company, a life insurance company that provides services to funeral homes, acquired most of eFuneral's assets in a deal that closed in early 2014. This the kind of acquisition you never read about in TechCrunch or VentureBeat because there were no press releases issued about it. This wasn't a "win" for anybody. It was simply a way for us to recoup *something* that we could return to investors. Ultimately, it was the final sentence in the last chapter for eFuneral. We failed.

Bouncing Back

One of the fears I had when we took the leap to launch eFuneral was what would happen if things didn't go the way that we planned. "What if we failed?" I wondered. Would we ever be able to convince investors to give us another shot at launching another startup? Would we even be able to find jobs? I've heard that failure can be seen as a badge of honor in a place like Silicon Valley, but what about Cleveland, Ohio? How would people there treat our startup failure?

The first taste of understanding how people might react was with a conversation I had with one of our investors. This person wasn't personally connected to us prior to eFuneral. He wasn't a mentor. He was an angel investor who simply learned about our business and thought it was one worth investing in. I broke the news to him that he wouldn't be seeing any return on his investment. His $20,000 essentially turned into thin air. His response? "Mike, you've kept me informed the entire time and there isn't one decision you made that I thought was a bad one. You did what you could, gave it your best shot, and I only hope you'll let me know about your next startup so I can invest in that one."

It turns out that when you fail at a startup, if you do things the right way and treat your investors and employees like partners throughout, you're not untouchable. In fact, Bryan and I personally saw opportunities open up for us after we wound eFuneral down that simply wouldn't have been available prior to eFuneral. We both went on to accept leadership roles at other local early stage companies. And we both believe that before too long, we'll be in a position to start another company of our own.

Cleveland didn't turn its back on us. It embraced us. The founders and investors in our startup community celebrated the daunting challenge we took on of attempting to build an innovative technology company in an antiquated market. They encouraged us to tell our story, and other founders still continue to turn to us to ask for guidance for their own startups.

It didn't take long for the rest of the eFuneral team to find some amazing opportunities, too. Within about 30 days of the meeting I never wanted to have, every single eFuneral team member had great job offers from other successful startup and early stage companies. It won't be long until each one of them launches their *own* startup company – I'm certain of it. I only hope that I can have the chance to work with them again.

Since winding down eFuneral, I've been invited to speak to college classes, startup events, and on podcasts to tell the eFuneral story. Each time, I'm always asked the same question: With everything you've gone through with eFuneral, will you do it all over again and launch another startup?

It doesn't take me very long to answer: Of course… when the time is right. In a way, this book was my own personal "startup" project, and I certainly hope that you feel like you're now better prepared to raise funding for your business – even if you are outside of Silicon Valley. I also hope that the additional context of hearing more about my personal story and the eFuneral story was useful as well.

I wish you the best of luck on *your* startup adventure. Don't forget to enjoy the journey.

APPENDIX

Thank you for investing your time into this book. By now, you've noticed that there are dozens of helpful websites, materials, and other resources that I referenced in the book. I've taken the time to capture these all in one place. To receive a copy of all of these resources, visit SeedFundingBook.com/FreeResources.

Also, you'll find more of my writing about startups at my blog OutsideOfTheValley.com.

Finally, I'd love to hear from you! Feel free to send any questions, feedback, or comments to me at mikebelsito@gmail.com.

DISCLAIMER

While the author has used his best efforts in preparing this book, he makes no representations or warranties with respect to the accuracy or completeness of the contents of the book. The advice and strategies in this book may not be suitable for your situation. You should consult a professional where appropriate. The author shall not be liable for any loss of profit or any other commercial damages, including but not limited to special, incidental, consequential, or other damages.

ABOUT THE AUTHOR

Mike Belsito is a startup business and product developer that loves creating something from nothing. Mike has been involved with startups as an early employee, founder, and leadership team member for the past 10 years. Mike was the Co-Founder of two companies that produced products featured by The New York Times, The Atlantic, CNN, and others. Mike is a regular speaker on entrepreneurship, is an advisor to several start-ups and accelerator programs, and writes frequently through his blog, Outside of the Valley. Mike also serves as Entrepreneur-in-Residence for his hometown, Lakewood, Ohio. Mike earned degrees from Case Western Reserve University (MBA) and Bowling Green State University.

ACKNOWLEDGMENTS

I wrote this book for "Mike Belsito circa 2010". It was at this point that I knew I would eventually start a business and could need venture funding, but I had no clue where to start. Five years later, after having gone through the process of raising nearly $1 Million for my own startup company, I realized that a book like this one could serve as a useful guide for others.

Yet, this book simply wouldn't have been possible without the help of so many others. First and foremost, I am so thankful for the support of my wife, Hannah, for allowing me to explore various entrepreneurial ventures and take our family on some wild rides. I'm also grateful for my son, Edison, for allowing his Daddy to work on this book. And, of course, the book wouldn't have been possible without Bryan Chaikin, who was not only a business partner, but continues to be a great friend. I'm already looking forward to our next startup together, whenever that may be.

There was also a team of people that were incredibly helpful throughout the editing process. First and foremost, I'd like to thank those who spent a great deal of time editing this book, including Lindsay Preston Friedman, Lynn-Ann Gries, and Jay Donovan. In different ways, they're responsible for helping turn loosely structured thoughts into a well-organized book.

I'd also like to thank the following individuals who agreed to provide feedback throughout the creation of this book, and as a result, helped create what the book became: Jay Apple, Jim Armour, Richard Bannister, Ashley Barile, Eric Beland, Laura Bennett, Zach Boerger, Stefan Bogdanovic, Ellery Bowker, Geoff Brash, John Braunstein, Gary Campion, Prakash Channagiri, Ron Copfer, Luis Cousin, Douglas Craver, Alessio D'Antino, Kevin DeFranco, Nikita Eelen, Cesar Fernandes, Alain Fontaine, Flor Franco, Robert Fridrich, Patti Glaza, Michael Goldberg, Nick Gory, Rakesh Guha, Geoff Hardman, John Hopper, Scott Huff, Lorie Jackson, Ed Jones, Paula Kampf,

Charles Knight, Gayrajain Kohli, Frank Kotsianas, Lokesh Kumar, Maria LaLonde, Ray Leach, Emil Lee, Kelcey Lehrich, Jonathan Lewis, Shannon Lyons, Dave Mariano, Michael Masello, Nichelle McCall, Dave McNamara, Anurag Mehrotra, Thomas Millay, Dan Moulthrop, Alvin Mullins, Amit Patel, Amlan Patnaik, Sean Peppard, Pramod Prasanth, Umair Rehman, Chad Rhyner, Philippe Rivard, Rich Rodman, Michael Sacca, Anurag Saxena, Zolt Seregi, Tony Sheng, Shubs Sheth, Max Snyder, Bob Sopko, Joan Soskin, Anthony Stedillie, Brad Steinberg, Scott Vinick, Jeremy Voros, Annal Vyas, Stefanie White, Adam Winter, Josh Womack, and Patrick Zhao.

I'd like to also thank other friends and family members that were instrumental in me writing this book, both knowingly and unknowingly: Rob Adams, Anthony Belsito, Catherine Belsito, Lynn Belsito, Suzanne Belsito, Michael Camp, Christopher Celeste, Bryan Chaikin, Scott Chaikin, Chip Chaikin, Dennis Cocco, Mary Beth Cooper, Rachel Fritzman, Mike Fritzman, Patty Fritzman, Matt Gaudio, Chelsea Gumucio, Ray Herschman, Kristin Hughes, Creg Jantz, Nancy Kramer, Mitch Kroll, Mike Lisavich, Paul Lee, Trevor Loy, Bob Maupin, Dianne Maupin, Paul McAvinchey, Kitty McDowell, Tim Mueller, Peter Nealis, Ryan O'Donnell, Kurt Pettit, Brian Phelps, Kim Sanchez Rael, Cliff Reynolds, Bob Roth, Leah Yomtovian Roush, Wil Schroter, Mark Schwartz, Ed Smith, Mark Smith, Charles Stack, Cheryl Strom, David Teten, Mike Trabert, Doug Weintraub, Ira Weiss, Stina Wing, Marko Zlatic, and Greg Zucca.

Finally, I'd like to thank those entrepreneurs and investors who allowed me to profile their stories and experiences in the book as well, including: Ed Buchholz, David Cohen, Alex Frommeyer, Blair Garrou, Robert Hatta, John Knific, Randy Komisar, Danielle Morrill, Tanisha Robinson, Tige Savage, Ian Sigalow, Blake Squires, Brian Trautschold, and Morris Wheeler.

Printed in Great Britain
by Amazon